D0464852

No SMALL Potatoes

Al Puser

No SMALL Potatoes

HOW A FAMILY POTATO SALAD RECIPE IS FAST BECOMING A BILLION DOLLAR BUSINESS

AL RESER
with
KERRY TYMCHUK

Oregon State University Alumni Association
Corvallis

Published for the Oregon State University Alumni
Association by Oregon State University Press

The paper in this book meets the guidelines for permanence
and durability of the Committee on Production Guidelines
for Book Longevity of the Council on Library Resources and
the minimum requirements of the American National Stan-
dard for Permanence of Paper for Printed Library Materials
Z39.48-1984.

Library of Congress Cataloging-in-Publication Data

Reser, Al, 1935-
  No small potatoes : how a family potato salad recipe is fast
becoming a billion dollar business / Al Reser, with Kerry
Tymchuk.
    p. cm.
  ISBN 978-0-87071-630-0 (alk. paper)
  1. Reser, Al, 1935- 2. Reser's Fine Foods--History.
3. Businessmen--Oregon--Biography. 4. Convenience
foods--Oregon--History. 5. Food industry and trade--
Oregon--History. I. Tymchuk, Kerry. II. Title.
  HD9010.R47A3 2010
  338.7'664009795--dc22
                                    2010012091

Oregon State University Press
121 The Valley Library
Corvallis OR 97331-4501
541-737-3166 • fax 541-737-3170
http://oregonstate.edu/dept/press

OREGON STATE UNIVERSITY ALUMNI ASSOCIATION

The OSU Alumni Association's mission is to be an indispensable part of Oregon State University by engaging alumni and friends in the life, promotion, and advancement of the university. Our vision is to enrich the lives of alumni and friends by helping them establish lifelong, meaningful, and valued relationships with OSU and with each other.

OSU Alumni Association
204 CH2M HILL Alumni Center
Corvallis, Oregon 97331
www.osualum.com

To Patricia

TABLE OF CONTENTS

FOREWORD

When Al Reser first mentioned to me that he was working on a book that would share his life story and the story of the billion-dollar business that started in his parents' farmhouse kitchen, two thoughts immediately crossed my mind.

The first was that this was a book I wanted to read, as I knew Al's life and career stood for the principle that good people can accomplish remarkable things. My second thought was that when the book was published, I couldn't wait to host a party honoring Al and his wife, Pat, as a small token of my respect for them and all they have done for Oregon State University, the magnificent institution I am privileged to lead.

How I wish I had the opportunity to host that party. Unfortunately, as readers of this book undoubtedly know, Al passed away in his sleep on April 12, 2010, while on a short vacation in Florida. His passing at the age of 74 was a profound loss to his family, his friends, his employees, his industry, his community, and everyone who, like Al, is proud to wear the orange and black of "Beaver Nation."

In the days before his passing, Al did spend many hours making his final changes and edits to the galley proofs of this book, and I know he was very proud of it.

Hardly a day has gone by since Al's passing when I have not thought of him and the values which he exuded: humility, philanthropy, generosity, authenticity. Those values, which were front and center in his life, are also front and center in *No Small Potatoes*. How Al rose from his impoverished childhood to preside over one of America's largest and most successful refrigerated-food businesses is a story that would make Horatio Alger envious, and one that will inspire all those who read it.

As proud as Al Reser was of OSU, I can report that OSU was even prouder of the example set and the legacy created by Al, Pat, and the entire Reser family.

Maya Angelou once wrote that "People will forget what you said, people will forget what you did, but people will never forget how you made them feel." Al Reser made people feel welcome, valued, and like family. The success of Reser's Fine Foods stems in no small part from the fact that all who work there were family to Al in every sense of the word. His capacity for giving was extraordinary, and as long as there is an Oregon State University, Al Reser will never be forgotten.

Dr. Ed Ray
President, Oregon State University

PROLOGUE

I remember it like it was yesterday. It was June 14, 1999. My wife, Pat, and I had returned to the campus of Oregon State University in Corvallis, Oregon, where we had both received our undergraduate degrees some forty years earlier. Four of our five children had followed in our footsteps and are also proud OSU graduates. Throughout the years, we had spent many autumn Saturdays rooting for the Beavers football team at Parker Stadium. While the stadium had remained essentially the same for decades, the changes in Pat's and my life had led us to a decision that would change the face of Oregon State University and the name of Parker Stadium.

Soon after graduating from OSU in 1960, I became president of "Mrs. Reser's Salads," a small business founded by my parents that made and sold potato, macaroni, and gelatin salads to supermarkets, grocery stores, delicatessens, and butcher shops in Oregon. The business, which began in 1950 at my mother's kitchen table, had slowly grown to the point a decade later where it boasted a dozen or so part-time employees and annual sales of three hundred thousand dollars.

"Wouldn't it be something," I said to Pat soon after my first day as president of the company, "if someday we could actually reach half a million dollars in annual sales?"

As Pat and I traveled to Corvallis that June day, we couldn't help but reflect on all that had occurred since I asked her that question. Reser's Fine Foods (I changed the name of the business soon after becoming president) had become one of the nation's leading manufacturers and distributors of refrigerated processed foods, offering some fifteen hundred products that were available in all fifty states, as well as in Canada and Mexico. Our more than sixteen hundred employees worked at fifteen separate production facilities that were located in seven states. And where I once hoped for $500,000 in sales each year, we now were achieving sales that averaged more than that every day, as our 1999 annual sales topped $250 million.

Pat and I knew that we were very blessed, and we had long believed in sharing our blessings by giving back to our community. Over the years, we watched with pride as Reser's Fine Foods sponsored a countless series of little league baseball and softball teams, donated products to food banks, and contributed to Special Olympics, Junior Achievement, St. Matthew Lutheran Church, and any number of philanthropic organizations. We also loyally supported Oregon State University, giving to a variety of academic and athletic programs at our alma mater. Still, we felt called to do more, and readily accepted when OSU administrators asked if they could meet with us to offer a suggestion on further involvement with the University.

They kicked off the meeting by reminding us that Parker Stadium was the smallest and oldest football field in the Pacific-10 Athletic Conference. They made it clear that if Oregon State University was to compete successfully with other universities in the conference, a major upgrade and renovation of the stadium would be required. Their suggestion was a simple one: if we would provide the funds for the renovation, they would honor our gift by renaming the facility "Reser Stadium."

Pat and I are fairly private people, and the idea of having our name—and our company's name—on the side of a stadium was more than a little intimidating. We understood that the increased attention the "Reser" name would receive would also mean increased scrutiny of our company and our family. Any misstep we made, no matter how small or how unintended, would reflect poorly—not just on us, but on OSU as well.

After much discussion and thought, Pat and I concluded that a "Reser Stadium" was a fitting way in which we could pay tribute to all those—our family, our employees, our suppliers, and our customers—who helped Reser's succeed beyond our wildest dreams.

So, on June 14, 1999, we joined with OSU administrators at a press conference where our gift was announced and the name "Reser Stadium" was officially unveiled. Pat and I made it clear that our gift was not just about football, as it is academics and not athletics that define a university. Our donation was about the entire university. It was about expressing confidence in leadership that was instigating exciting changes at OSU, and raising the awareness of OSU throughout the nation.

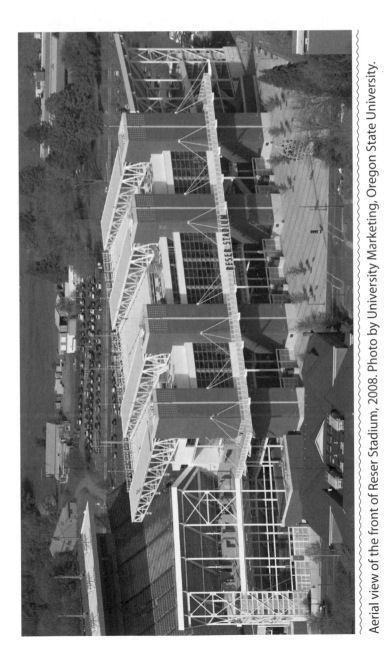

Aerial view of the front of Reser Stadium, 2008. Photo by University Marketing, Oregon State University.

More than a decade has passed since Pat and I made that donation, and we haven't regretted it for a moment. Since 1999, the fortunes of the OSU Beavers football team have dramatically improved, and they have attended post-season bowl games in nine consecutive seasons, winning six of those. The Beavers baseball team, playing on the recently expanded Goss field, won back-to-back NCAA national championships in 2006 and 2007. With the addition of the Linus Pauling Science Center and a reputation as a national leader in many areas of scientific research, OSU has continued to hit home runs in scholarship, as well.

While Reser's Fine Foods can't claim the title of "national champions," I can report that the years since 1999 have been ones of exciting growth. Our workforce has increased from 1,600 to 2,600 and annual sales have more than doubled from $250 million to over $700 million. We continue to be recognized as an innovative company that trusts and rewards its employees, that gives back to our community, that raises the standards of our industry, and that offers American families a constantly expanding variety of great-tasting salads, side dishes, snacks, dips, Mexican foods, and desserts at a fair price.

Though I have reached what most people consider "retirement age," you can find me at our headquarters most every day, as I continue to serve as Chief Executive Officer and Chairman of the Board of Reser's. Why? Well, the food business continues to fascinate me; I am motivated to help Reser's reach a billion dollars in annual sales; and I love working with my three sons, who all have offices just down the hall from mine.

I do leave for home a little bit earlier than I used to, and I am enjoying more vacations with Pat and more time spent with our grandchildren. I also found the time to finally do what family, friends, and colleagues have long urged me to do—to share the remarkable story of Reser's Fine Foods. It is a story that proves that small potatoes and big dreams are a perfect recipe for success.

ONE

iven that I've spent most of my life in the food business, I've always thought it fitting that my mother and father met each other in a restaurant.

The fact that my mother, Mildred Smith, was waitressing in a Wichita, Kansas restaurant in 1932 was testimony to the number of lives that were turned upside down by the Great Depression. Born in 1912, my mother spent her first eighteen years growing up in relative privilege. Her father owned a very successful Kansas grain-elevator operation, which gave him the means to provide his family with a maid, a cook, and the prestige of owning the first car in town.

My mother was attending college when the 1929 Stock Market Crash sent countless American families—including hers—into bankruptcy. With her father suddenly unable to afford tuition, my mother soon entered the workforce, playing the violin at silent-movie theaters, and waitressing at a number of restaurants.

My father, Earl Reser, did not have as far to fall when the bottom dropped out of the economy. Born in 1913, he was orphaned before he was a teenager, and was without a real home for many years, as he shuffled among relatives. After turning eighteen, he attempted to survive the Depression by roaming from town to town in search of any business that was hiring. Eventually he landed in Wichita—and happened into the restaurant where Mildred Smith was working.

After a short courtship, my mother and father were married in January 1934. They had another mouth to feed when I was born in Topeka on May 27, 1935. My three sisters, Lois, Phyllis, and Dodie, would be added to the family over the course of the next ten years.

There's an old saying that success in business is due to equal parts of inspiration and perspiration. Those qualities have been key to the success of Reser's Fine Foods, and I suppose it can be said that I inherited the inspiration gene from my father, and the perspiration gene from my mother.

My dad was a dreamer and a natural salesman who always had a new business idea or promotion up his sleeve. My mother was the practical one. She understood from her personal experience that success could be fleeting, and that there was no substitute for hard work. And there was no doubt about it—raising a family during some incredibly tough economic times definitely required hard work.

Much of my childhood was spent on the move, as Dad had a severe case of wanderlust, believing that the Depression would end and better days could be found just down the road. Many of my earliest memories involve packing and moving, as my parents took us from Kansas to Colorado to Oregon and back again to Kansas in search of economic stability. As a result of these constant comings and goings, I attended seven different grade schools in eight years, and there were times when I never seemed to be on the same page as my classmates.

Occasionally, one of my dad's ideas panned out, and our cupboards were temporarily full. For a while, he operated the "Reser Fruit Stand" in Topeka, and I remember walking home from third grade one day in 1943 and seeing a massive traffic jam in town. I was amazed to discover that the cause of the traffic jam was Dad, who was selling fresh plums from the back of a semi-truck. Plums, like all fresh fruits, were almost impossible to find during the rationing days of World War II, and when word got out that my father had somehow obtained a shipment, it seemed as if all of Kansas lined up.

Dad also achieved some temporary success operating a small trucking business in the final years of World War II. His main customer was the U.S. government, which contracted with him to haul food to local military bases. I recall accompanying Dad in the truck on a few deliveries to the base, which also operated as a prison camp for German soldiers who had been shipped to the United States. I couldn't help but recall photos I had seen of emaciated Allied prisoners in German camps, and was proud that our country treated prisoners with more dignity.

Between the occasional profitable ventures, however, were the far more frequent months when Dad's latest idea would not work out, and we would pack up our apartment late at night and move out of town, literally one step ahead of the bill collectors. My mother managed the family money during good times and bad, and somehow she saved just enough to keep my sisters and me from going hungry.

One of my mother's staples in keeping food in our family's stomach was her potato salad. While I can't remember the first time I tasted it, I can remember that I sure ate a lot of it growing up. It was relatively cheap to make, and eventually it dawned on my mother that while she was making some for her family, she might also be able to make some for other families. In the summer of 1943 she began to make and package potato salad in our small kitchen, and my father would sell it to a few old-fashioned meat markets in Topeka. They didn't make any large sales, but every dollar helped the family pocketbook.

My father's constant search for greener pastures led us to Oregon in 1945, when he accepted an opportunity to work in the logging business with one of his relatives. Having lived most of my young life on the flat plains of Kansas, I was astonished by the Pacific Northwest landscape, its tall trees and taller mountains. We made our home right in the middle of a thick, green forest, in an area called Dixie Mountain near the small Columbia County community of Scappoose. Our small house had no electricity, no running water, and our nearest neighbor was a quarter mile away. My daily chores included cutting wood, which we used for heating and cooking, and filling barrels with water from a nearby spring and tying them to a sled, which our horse, "Babe," would pull back to the house. More often than not, one of the barrels tumbled off the sled, spilling all the water, and Babe and I would have to head back to the spring to refill the barrel.

I am sure that most people would have considered my time at Dixie Mountain a lonely, meager, and miserable existence. It probably was all that, but as I look back on it, it was also a tremendous learning experience that taught me many lessons about the importance of perseverance and hard work.

Along with my chores, I also hoped to contribute to the family finances by getting a job. My cousin and I managed to get hired by a local railroad to work as dishwashers in a kitchen they operated to feed the men who worked on their tracks. It didn't take me long to figure out that the cook liked to drink more than he liked to cook, and many evenings he would head off to the local tavern and not return. I had picked up a pointer or two by watching my mother in the kitchen, and soon found myself spending more time preparing the food and less time washing the dishes.

The logging business didn't pan out for my dad, so we eventually left Oregon, landing briefly in Colorado before moving on to Stockton, Kansas. Still not yet a teenager, I worked the following summer pulling twelve-hour shifts as the night cook in a small restaurant. Things would get really hectic around four o'clock every morning, when seventy or so men on their way to the oil fields would stop in for sack lunches. The waitress, dishwasher, and I would operate as an assembly line, as we packed three sandwiches, two cookies, a piece of pie, a piece of fresh fruit, and a candy bar in each sack. I also made a lot of hamburgers and meat loaf and quickly learned that our supply of ground beef would last longer if you mixed in some breadcrumbs with the meat. When a customer only half-joked that he didn't need any bread for his sandwich because there was enough in the meat, I realized I probably was overdoing the breadcrumbs. A friend and I also picked up some extra money by cooking hot dogs at the restaurant, loading them on our bicycles, and peddling down to the local ball field where we would sell them to spectators watching summer baseball games.

Despite our best efforts, the family financial situation was worse than ever when I completed my eighth-grade year in the summer of 1949. Dad decided to move the family once again to Oregon, and we packed up what little we owned and headed back to the Pacific Northwest. After paying for gas and food on the road we arrived in Oregon in August 1949 with precisely $1.20 in Dad's wallet. The only accommodations we could afford were in a labor camp in the Washington County community of Hillsboro, where we were charged rent of $5 a week.

The labor camp was a series of small wood structures which really weren't more than one-room shacks. The furniture consisted of a wood-burning stove, a sink, a table, four chairs, and two sets of bunk beds. Bathrooms and showers were located in another structure and were shared with other residents of the camp. It certainly wasn't much, but since we slept in our car during the trip from Kansas to Oregon, I was grateful for it.

With rent to be paid and food to be bought, every member of the family was expected to pitch in. Thankfully, the rich soil of Washington County made the area a hub of agricultural activity. Dad and I quickly found work picking corn for sixty cents an hour, and Mom and Lois picked beans. Phyllis babysat Dodie.

Picking corn was dusty and backbreaking work. I especially remember one day when, as part of a picking crew, Dad and I were throwing corn into the back of a large truck that slowly traveled alongside us. I was walking at the side of the truck, and two times in an hour I accidentally threw the corn through the truck's open window, striking the driver in the head. After the second occurrence, the driver jumped out of the truck, and ran at me with a raised fist. I was certain he was about to hit me, but my dad stepped in and calmed him down. From then on, I was relegated to walking behind the truck, where there was no danger of one of my errant throws hitting anyone.

I began my freshman year at Hillsboro High School in September, 1949. The school required my home address for their records, and—embarrassed by my family's living conditions—I wrote down the address of a home down the road from the labor camp. To ensure that no one would doubt me, I got the school bus to pick me up each morning and drop me off each afternoon in front of that house.

Thankfully, a few months after our arrival, my parents were both hired by a local grocery store—Dad's job was produce manager, and Mom worked in the delicatessen department. Later they were both hired at Billy Bo's, a local Chinese restaurant. I would join them there for a time, cooking American food after school and on weekends.

The steady employment did allow our family to leave the labor camp in November and we rented a small cabin. After where we had lived, the cabin felt like a mansion. In reality, however, our "mansion" consisted of a tiny living room, a kitchen, a bathroom, and two bedrooms. Mom and Dad had one bedroom, my three sisters shared another, and I slept on the couch in the living room.

My wardrobe for school consisted of one pair of jeans, two shirts, one sweater, and one pair of penny loafers. My mother would wash my jeans in the middle of the week; she put them in the oven to ensure that they would be dry by the morning.

My penny loafers became an issue when I wore them during try-outs for the high school football team. I made the team, and continued to wear the shoes at football practices. After a few weeks of practice, the coach took me aside and explained that if I wanted a permanent spot on the team, I needed to buy real football shoes. The problem was that football shoes cost twelve dollars at the local hardware and sporting goods store—much more than my parents or I could afford. The coach said that the best he could do was to give me one week to find the money necessary to buy some shoes, and if I didn't, then I was off the team. I loved football and enjoyed being a member of a team, so I quickly developed a plan to get those shoes on my feet.

Step one of my plan was a job selling the local newspaper, the *Hillsboro Argus*, every Tuesday and Thursday afternoon after school. The paper sold for three cents a copy, and my commission was a penny for every copy I sold. I was also allowed to keep any tips, and was delighted that most people would pay me with a nickel and tell me to "keep the change," allowing me to make three cents for every paper I sold. I received a lesson in economics when the price of the *Argus* was raised to five cents and my commission was raised by a penny. Any thoughts I had that a raise in commission would mean more money in my pocket were eliminated—most customers would still pay with a nickel, leaving me with no tip and just my new two-cent commission for every paper sold.

Step two on completing my shoe account occurred to me when I happened upon a stash of beer bottles that residents of the labor camp had thrown into a nearby blackberry bramble. I cut a hole in the bramble, set some boards down to protect my knees and legs from the thorns, and spent hours on end carefully removing all the bottles I could reach. I would then cart them to a local grocery store, where I was paid a penny a bottle.

My Grandpa Smith—"Gramps," as everyone called him—had a favorite saying he would often share with me: "Watch the pennies and the dollars will take care of themselves." By following that advice, and by watching and saving and pinching every penny, I was able to go to my coach a week later with six dollars—half of the price of the shoes I needed to keep playing football. Maybe he was impressed with my industriousness, or maybe he just needed an eager offensive and defensive lineman; whatever the reason, the coach agreed to loan me the other six dollars of the purchase price of the shoes, and said I could pay him back as I continued to collect pennies. There was, however, still one big problem: the only pair of football shoes remaining at the store were size twelve, and I was a size ten! Undeterred, I got the shoes and played the entire season with paper stuffed in them, so they wouldn't fly off in the middle of the game.

Despite our precarious financial situation, Mom and Dad were able to keep us from going hungry, and my sisters and I could always count on filling up with Mom's potato salad. As she had done when we lived in Kansas, she began to use any free time to make larger and larger portions of her potato salad in our tiny kitchen, and Dad would go door-to-door at local butcher shops, delis, and grocery stores, offering samples to the managers, and asking them to offer "Mrs. Reser's Salads" to their customers. The flavor of my mom's salad and the considerable salesmanship skills of my dad led to sales large enough to enable us to move out of our cabin and into a rented farmhouse in nearby Cornelius, Oregon.

The farmhouse kitchen was much larger than the one at the cabin, and before long, there was water boiling and potatoes cooking on two burners on the kitchen stove and three or four more propane burners on the back porch. On a good day, with help from my sisters and me and our new next-door neighbor, Ida Vandehey, Mom could produce two hundred pounds of potato salad. The extra room also allowed Mom to add macaroni salad to her "product line."

I scrubbed floors, helped in salad preparation, and accompanied my father in making deliveries to local stores. At that time, refrigerated trucks were fairly new and much more expensive than my parents could afford, so we used dry ice and blankets to keep the salads cold as we made our deliveries. I did almost every job, with the exception of one: perhaps it was just youthful shyness; perhaps I was afraid of rejection; but whatever the reason, I was mortified at the thought of actually asking a store manager to buy some of our potato or macaroni salad. If I went along with my father or mother on sales calls, I would happily remain in the car while they went inside. That all changed one summer day when I was sixteen years old. My mother and I pulled up outside a small grocery store in the community of Oregon City. She turned the engine off, but instead of getting out, she just sat in the driver's seat.

"Are you going in?" I asked her.

"No," she replied. "You are."

I swallowed hard. "Are you going with me?" I asked.

"No," she said.

Any thought I had that she might be bluffing was set aside when she pulled out a book from her purse and began to read. "The store doesn't close for a few more hours," she said with a smile. "You take your time and I'll just stay here and read."

After sitting in the car for what seemed like an hour in a failed effort to calm my nerves, I finally opened the door and stepped outside. I walked around the store several times before actually going in. I located the manager, offered him a taste of our salads, and almost hugged him when he said that he would buy twelve containers of potato salad and six containers of macaroni salad at thirty cents a container. I have made countless sales calls since then—some worth millions of dollars—but no sale stands out in my memory more than that $5.40 sale in Oregon City!

I don't recall why my mother was the one who walked into the brand new Hillsboro Safeway supermarket in 1951 to ask if they were interested in buying her potato salad—making the sales pitch to stores was usually my father's job—but I'm sure glad she did it. The manager tasted her potato salad, and asked my mother a question she never expected: Could she supply potato salad to not just the Hillsboro store but to every Safeway store in Oregon? Probably without knowing exactly whether or not she could actually do what she was being asked, and certainly not knowing that her response would set her small potato salad business on the path to becoming the nation's leading salad manufacturer, she said "Yes."

TWO

What is it about my mother's potato salad that motivated Safeway to order it for all their Oregon stores, that has made it Reser's most popular item for over half a century, and that has led to countless letters and e-mails from folks declaring it the "best they have ever tasted?" Believe me, I have asked myself that question many times, and I still don't know the answer. Perhaps it's the fact that she used—and we continue to use—Russet potatoes, which are consistently flavorful and have good texture. Perhaps it's our combination of vinegar and spices that are a perfect blend of sweet and tart.

What I do know is that if you enter the words "potato salad recipes" into an Internet search engine, you are informed that there are more than two hundred thousand links! Thankfully for Reser's, potato salad has become part of the American culture, and it's almost unpatriotic to host a Fourth of July barbecue without it.

I also know that different regions of our country have different tastes and demand different potato salads. As a result, we now mix over ninety potato salad recipes that reflect these regional differences, including Southern Mustard Potato Salad, Amish Potato Salad, Creole Potato Salad, German Potato Salad, and Northwest Potato Salad.

(A complete list of all Reser's potato salads is printed at the end of this book.)

My parents didn't have time to dream what the future would hold when Mom agreed to Safeway's request. They were far too busy dealing with the present, which included the fact that it was impossible to make all the potato salad necessary to fill the order in our farmhouse kitchen. That conclusion was reinforced when some gentlemen in suits and ties showed up on our doorstep. They identified themselves as representatives from Borden's, which was one of the leading food companies of the time, famous for their evaporated milk and their corporate image of "Elsie the Cow."

They had seen Mrs. Reser's Salads products in local stores, tasted them, were impressed by them, and wanted to talk to my dad about him producing some salads under the "Borden's" label. A local store owner had apparently told them the location of our farmhouse, and they told my dad that they would be interested in touring his manufacturing plant. Not wanting to tell them that the "plant" was actually our kitchen, Dad told them the plant was closed for the day, and he took them to a downtown restaurant for a cup of coffee. Before their meeting was over, Dad had agreed to produce some potato, macaroni, coleslaw, and gelatin salads for Borden's.

Within a matter of weeks, the Reser family and the Reser business relocated to a two-story building in downtown Cornelius. The office and storage for "Mrs. Reser's Salads" took up the front ten feet of the first story, and production and packaging took up the rest. Our living quarters were in an apartment on the second floor.

A larger workforce was also needed to fill the new orders, and my parents hired another half-dozen or so of their friends to help in the process of manually cooking, peeling, and dicing potatoes, mixing salad ingredients, and packaging salads in paper cups. There were no regular hours. If there was work to be done and an order to be filled, you just had to be there—even if it was midnight.

Summer was by far the busiest time for Mrs. Reser's Salads. In the 1950s there was a definite "salad season," lasting from Memorial Day until Labor Day. No matter how hard my parents tried, they couldn't convince many grocers or delis that their customers would enjoy potato and macaroni salads in the fall, winter, or spring. As a result, the business was almost entirely dependent on profits made in the summer months to tide it over for the remainder of the year. In fact, there were some years when nearly one-third of annual sales were achieved during the week of July 4th.

There was always lots of work to be done during those summer months, but I also remember that there was lots of fun to be had. The employees were our friends and neighbors, and my parents treated them as such. What was most enjoyable for me was seeing my parents finally achieve a degree of success. For the first sixteen years of my life, I had watched as they struggled each day just to make ends meet. The new and encouraging signs of success for Mrs. Reser's Salads had not made them rich by any stretch of the imagination, but it gave them hope and optimism that a better life was ahead.

With high school graduation fast approaching, I had to decide what the future held for me. Attending college was an option I had never really envisioned, as I far preferred playing football or working for my parents than hitting the books. Still, I had managed to pass all my classes, and in May 1953 I received my diploma from Hillsboro High School. I can still vividly recall the feeling that hit me as I marched down the aisle in cap and gown to "Pomp and Circumstance." It was the somewhat surprising realization that I wanted to hear that music again. Then and there, I quietly resolved to myself that one day I would earn a college diploma.

My immediate future, however, involved enlisting in the United States Army. The Korean War was ongoing, and along with many others from my generation, I felt a calling to serve my country. So, in December 1953, I said good-bye to my family and friends and boarded a train for Fort Ord in beautiful Monterey Bay, California. I arrived at Fort Ord with no idea whether or not I would be sent to Korea after completing basic training. As it turned out, it was during my basic training when peace negotiations began in earnest. As a result, no additional troops would be sent to Korea. Instead of traveling overseas, I ended up in the kitchens and mess halls of a variety of military bases, since my culinary experience qualified me for Army Cook School.

I was first assigned to Fort Lewis in Pierce County, Washington, and then sent on to Fort Bragg in North Carolina. Military kitchens were not blessed with the most modern of equipment, and most of my work was accomplished on huge and temperamental coal-heated stoves. Feeding the six hundred men in our company led to many long days and nights of kneading and rolling what seemed like the acres of dough necessary to make enough sweet rolls and dinner rolls to satisfy the hungry soldiers. It was hard work, but I didn't mind it—if I wasn't in the kitchen, I was expected to be marching with the troops!

After precisely two years and one day in the military, I received my discharge papers and returned to Oregon in December 1955. My time in the military provided me both with the maturity to conclude that I was ready for college, and the GI Bill benefits that enabled me to afford the tuition at Portland State College, where I enrolled in classes beginning in January 1956.

One of my dad's many business efforts was a fruit stand in Topeka, Kansas. This ad is from the *Topeka State Journal* in October, 1943.

With our family budget always tight, I wore the same pair of overalls countless times!

Mom, Dad, Lois, Phyllis, and me. Dodie would complete the family several years later.

A Hillsboro labor camp was our first home in Oregon. The quality of the photograph matches the quality of the housing.

To add to the family's income, Mom makes potato salad in the family kitchen starting in 1950.

Potato salad production started in earnest in a small production facility in Cornelius.

My mom (left) and Nellie Jacques, one of Reser's first employees. My mother never dreamed that her potato salad would be the start of a billion dollar business.

High school graduation in 1953.

I worked and saved so I could afford the football shoes necessary to play at Hillsboro High School. I am third from the left on the top row.

One of our early billboard advertisements. The "Dutch girl" is a tribute to the Dutch heritage of the Reser name.

The "potato room" in 1959. Most of the early Reser's employees were friends or neighbors of my parents.

My years in the army—more valuable life lessons learned!

The smartest decision I ever made was to marry Patricia in 1958.

We received our diplomas from OSU in 1960, two years after exchanging wedding vows.

My Dad (left), Darrell Vandehey, and I continuing a Reser family tradition of innovation, creating a new product line.

THREE

hanks to the GI Bill, there were quite a few Korean War veterans enrolled at Portland State College. Many of us had been out of the classroom for a while, and it didn't take long for some of us to determine that we could use some help with our assignments and homework. And if that help just happened to come from a lovely co-ed, then so much the better. Some of my buddies even suggested a contest to see who could get that "help" first, decreeing that we would all simultaneously break up with our "study partners" at the end of the semester, freeing us up to date someone else.

It wasn't a very honorable scheme. And after precisely one date with Pat Valian I knew that I didn't want the "help" to end. I first saw Pat in an English class that was intended for students who had a less-than-stellar academic record. My high-school transcript justified my being there, but Pat was an excellent student. A clerical error in the registrar's office had placed her in the class, and when the teacher determined she didn't belong there, he told her she should transfer to a more challenging class. Pat declined, thinking to herself that she had been placed there for a reason. I continue to thank my lucky stars that, as it turned out, I was that reason.

It took me a while to get up the nerve to ask Pat out on a date, but I finally resolved to do it one day after class, and I paced in the hallway outside the classroom, waiting for her to emerge. Unbeknownst to me, the professor had asked her to stay after class for a moment, so he could warn her of his suspicions that an army veteran was showing an interest in her, and recommend to her that she should steer clear of him. Fortunately, she rejected his advice and accepted my offer of a date. (Five years later, while Pat and I were on vacation with our first two children in Vancouver, British Columbia, we bumped into that professor, and Pat delighted in introducing me as the GI he had warned her about!)

Pat was—and is—beautiful, bright, and fun. If it wasn't love at first sight for me, it was pretty darn close. We began seeing each other in the fall of 1956 at Portland State, and were married June 18, 1958, at the close of our sophomore year. We transferred to Oregon State University in Corvallis that fall.

Along with the promises we made to each other in our wedding vows, we also made three pledges concerning what would occur in our life together. First, we agreed that both of us would graduate from college before we began a family. (We just missed keeping this pledge—our first child, Marty, was born 10 days before our graduation from OSU.) Second, we agreed that as long as I was working in my parents' business, Pat would not. I had seen on numerous occasions how my parents brought their work problems and disagreements home with them, and I didn't want any part of that. Also, Pat was getting her degree in elementary education, and her passion was clearly for teaching, not the food business. Finally, we agreed that no matter where we worked or what we did—for richer, for poorer, for better, for worse—we would always give back to our community. We wondered, however, if we would ever have anything to give, as we paid all our college and living expenses out of the $135 a month stipend I received under the GI Bill. (I often joked with Pat that one of the reasons I married her was because as a single man I only received a monthly benefit of $110, whereas married students got $25 more.)

There were weeks during the first year of our marriage when it seemed that Pat and I barely saw each other. We were both juggling a full load of classes—Pat focused on earning her teaching degree, and I was mixing business classes with an occasional course in food technology—and we would spend most evenings studying in the library. If I wasn't hitting the books, I was devoting my time to Mrs. Reser's Salads, where my parents still depended on my weekend help.

Most Friday nights, I would get home from the library late in the evening, and immediately hop in the car and make the two-hour drive from Corvallis to Cornelius, so I could start work first thing Saturday morning. Truth be told, the drive didn't bother me that much, because I was able to make it in the 1955 Pontiac I had bought when I returned home from the military. I've always been a car buff, and this big sea-foam-green two-door hardtop sedan was the first car I ever bought. Boy, did I love it! If you promise not to tell Pat, I will let you in on a little secret: sometimes on those lonely Oregon country roads I could get the speedometer up to 90 miles an hour.

My summer months were busy ones, spent in the kitchen of Mrs. Reser's Salads, in grocery stores trying to sell our products, or in trucks delivering them. It didn't take a degree in business administration to know that having the vast majority of your sales and your revenue occur during June, July, and August was not a formula for long-term success, and whenever I went into a grocery store I would find myself walking up and down the aisles, carefully inspecting different displays and searching for a product idea that would provide Mrs. Reser's Salads with a revenue stream that would continue beyond the summer. In 1959, I was fortunate enough to discover that product. It's a product that was key to Reser's survival, and that has continued to be a market success for half a century.

But to tell the story correctly of how this product came to be, I need to begin with an event that occurred over a century earlier, in a kitchen on the other side of the country. In the summer of 1853, George Crum was working as a chef at Moon Lake Lodge, an elegant resort located in Saratoga Springs, New York. The lodge's menu included French-fried potatoes, which Crum prepared in the thick-cut style first popularized in France in the 1700s. One evening, a customer sent Crum's potatoes back, complaining they were too soggy and thick. Crum cut and fried a thinner batch, but the customer sent those back, as well.

Frustrated, Crum decided to slice the potatoes so thin and crisp that they couldn't possibly be eaten with a fork. Much to Crum's surprise, the customer loved the new creation. "Saratoga Chips" quickly became the most popular item on the lodge's menu, and they were soon being packaged and sold across New York and New England.

These potato "chips" remained a small specialty item until two events occurred in the 1920s. First, the mechanical potato-peeling machine was invented, making it possible to produce "Saratoga Chips" in large quantities. Second, a salesman named Herman Lay began to travel the southern United States in his car, selling chips to small grocers from Atlanta to Tennessee. By 1944, Lay's Potato Chips were being sold across the country, and the potato chip was well on its way to becoming one of America's favorite snack foods.

Sometime in the 1950s, more and more Americans decided that if there was anything better than a potato chip, it was a potato chip topped with a flavored "dip." A number of companies began to manufacture and sell these dips, which usually consisted of a small block of cream cheese and a packet of spices. The customer was required to mix the spices with the cream cheese. A relatively short shelf life and the fact that it took a great deal of beating and whipping to get the cream cheese soft enough so that the potato chip wouldn't immediate break into pieces when "dipped" prevented the product from gaining even greater popularity. The more I looked at these dips, the more I began to wonder if there wasn't some way to create a more "customer-friendly" and "chip-friendly" product—one that was softer and creamier, that didn't need to be mixed by the customer, that wouldn't cause the potato chip to break, and that had a longer shelf life.

Soon, I was spending any free hours I had in the kitchen, experimenting with different recipes and flavors. I decided to soften the dips by using sour cream as the base, rather than cream cheese. I was encouraged when the chips dipped in these samples emerged unbroken. In need of more expertise than just my own, I called on the OSU Food Technology Department for assistance. The professors made some suggestions to my recipe and arranged for panels of students to come in and serve as taste testers. Based on their input, I tinkered with my recipes, and settled on seven different flavors for the dip: Clam, Garlic, Blue Cheese, Onion, and French Onion—all of which were also traditional flavors for cream cheese–based dips—and two new flavors: Horseradish and Dill Pickle. By the summer of 1959, my parents and I began to consider whether or not we had the capability to successfully manufacture, sell, and distribute a brand-new product.

Our thought process took an unexpected turn shortly before the July 4th holiday. My parents, exhausted by the process of making enough salads to meet the holiday-weekend demand, were away for a few days of vacation. I was alone in the Cornelius office when Tom Ray, a representative from the Blue Bell Potato Chip Company happened to stop by. At the time, Blue Bell was the dominant snack-food company in the Pacific Northwest, with a sales, marketing, and distribution force that covered supermarkets and grocery stores in Oregon, Washington, Idaho, Montana, and northern California. The representative said that Blue Bell management was impressed with our potato and macaroni salads. They were always looking to expand their product lines, and wondered if we were working on anything new that might be of interest to them.

I'm sure my eyes about popped out of my head when I heard that question. "Yes," I finally said. "We just happen to be working on something new." I grabbed some samples from the refrigerator, and told him of my new recipe for potato-chip dip. He liked what he tasted, and asked if we would be interested in providing dips to Blue Bell, which they would sell under their label.

Under normal circumstances, this was a question that should have been directed to my parents. After all, the business was theirs. But they weren't there. I knew that Blue Bell's size and strength would unquestionably allow them to achieve far greater sales than my parents could ever have hoped to achieve on their own. I assured the Blue Bell representative that we would be very interested—an assurance my parents quickly endorsed upon their return.

Blue Bell wanted the new dips to hit the grocery-store shelves on October 1, so the next three months were a whirlwind of activity. I again tinkered with the recipes, as Blue Bell wanted the horseradish dip to be a little hotter and the blue-cheese dip to be a little chunkier. There were ingredients and packaging materials to be ordered in quantities larger than Mrs. Reser's Salads had ever ordered before, and we had to devise a way to keep such large quantities of ingredients from spoiling (the advent of refrigerated warehouses was still years in the future). Eventually, we arrived at a system where we stored 400-pound barrels of sour cream in a room filled with crushed ice. I also had to think about hiring and training additional employees, since our small workforce wasn't nearly large enough to produce all the dip that Blue Bell had ordered. I worked nearly around the clock on these tasks during July and August, and after the fall semester began at OSU, I returned to Cornelius every Friday, staying through the weekend.

Finally, in late September, it was time for production to begin. I found about ninety percent of my workforce at Pacific University, a small, private liberal-arts college in nearby Forest Grove, knowing from personal experience that college students were always in need of some extra money. I asked three or four members of the crew to come in on Friday afternoon, and we would make sure everything was in place. Additional workers arrived in the early evening to begin a manufacturing and packaging process that would continue non-stop for over forty straight hours until Sunday afternoon, when we would deliver the cases of dip to the Blue Bell warehouse.

While I was focusing my attention on the manufacturing process, the folks at Blue Bell were planning and implementing a very aggressive advertising and marketing campaign aimed at ensuring that consumers would give our new product a try. Full-page ads had been running for weeks in newspapers across the Northwest, announcing the introduction of Blue Bell dips. Eye-catching displays were also set up in countless grocery stores and supermarkets. The ads and displays offered consumers a great deal: anyone who mailed in five lids from the new dips would receive $2.50 from Blue Bell. Since the retail price of each container was usually a few pennies under fifty cents, customers could actually make a few pennies by taking advantage of the promotion. Not surprisingly, the mail room at Blue Bell headquarters was soon flooded with thousands upon thousands of lids. What was scheduled to be a six-week promotion was quickly cut back to four weeks. Even without the promotion, sales of the dips remained strong throughout autumn, easily surpassing Blue Bell's expectations and ensuring that I would continue to spend most weekends helping in Cornelius.

A few years later, Blue Bell was purchased by the Sunshine Biscuit Company, which made the decision to get out of the dip business, because their delivery trucks were not refrigerated. I made the decision to continue to manufacture the dip—and to sell it under the Reser's label. Half a century later, it is still the best-selling dip in Oregon, and we are working hard to make it one of the best-selling in the nation.

As I neared graduation from Oregon State University, I wrestled with the decision on what to do after receiving my diploma. Working with my parents was certainly an option. The "food business" was in my blood. During my study sessions in the college library, I would often wander over to the periodical section, and read food-industry trade journals. I was also proud of my potato-chip dip and its early success. Still, there was something holding me back. Maybe it was the fact that even with the increased revenue from our contract with Blue Bell, Mrs. Reser's Salads was still little more than a break-even proposition. Maybe it was the fact that Pat was pregnant, and I thought supporting a family required a job in a field that was more reliable. Whatever the reason, I determined that I would not join the family business. I had enjoyed a number of accounting classes at PSU and OSU, and had even served as the first president of the OSU Chapter of Beta Alpha Psi, a national accounting honorary organization. With the encouragement and advice of some of my professors, I decided that a career as an accountant would provide my soon-to-be growing family with a degree of stability.

I interviewed with a number of firms in the west and received several job offers. I decided to accept an offer from a small firm in Portland that had helped my parents with their books. Pat and I and newborn Marty moved to a Portland suburb, and I readied myself for my first day on the job. As it happened, my first day on the job was precisely two weeks before my last day on the job. To put it simply, I was bored stiff. Creating and introducing a new product into the market had challenged my ingenuity and my imagination, and I had enjoyed it a great deal. There was, however, little use for creativity in the accounting work I was assigned, and my eyes would glaze over as I tried to wade through a sea of numbers. There was no doubt about it: my heart and soul were still in the food business.

My resignation from the accounting firm came at a precipitous time for Mrs. Reser's Salads. My father had lived in the Hillsboro-Cornelius area for eleven years—the longest he had ever stayed in one place. And after years of living and working together around the clock, my parent's marriage had hit a rough spot that would eventually lead to their divorce. As a result, Dad decided that he would move on his own to Seattle and start a food-brokerage business, while my mother stayed behind. I borrowed some money from Grandpa Smith to buy Dad out of his share of the business, and in October 1960, at twenty-five years of age and just a few months out of college, I was the new president of Mrs. Reser's Salads.

FOUR

esides being asked if I would share my recipe for potato salad, the question I am most frequently asked is my recipe for succeeding in business. How did it happen? How did Reser's Fine Foods grow from $300,000 in annual sales in 1960 to over $700 million in annual sales today? How did Reser's survive and prosper through the 1960s and '70s, when countless other similar food-industry companies failed? What is the secret of running a family business without ruining your business or your family?

As I reflected back on the past half-century in an attempt to answer those questions, it became clear to me that "Reser's recipe for success" is a combination of many ingredients. Start with heaping portions of the most important ingredient—great people. Add generous amounts of perseverance and hard work. Combine with a core set of principles—like a passion for innovation, a commitment to quality, and a dedication to the needs of your customers. Mix with a habit of making the right decisions at critical moments. That is the recipe that has allowed Reser's to succeed. And that is the recipe that I know will continue to be passed down with care from generation to generation in the Reser family.

In the next chapters, I will share some specific examples of the people, the principles, and the decisions that have played an especially important role in the history of Reser's.

Potato Salad in the Big Apple: Taking Reser's Public

During my first days as president in the fall of 1960, I made a list of the assets of Reser's: a small building in Cornelius, a few pieces of machinery and equipment, some office furniture, a handful of delivery trucks, and a dozen or so full- or part-time employees, including my mother, my grandfather, and my sister Lois. Our product line consisted of potato, macaroni, and gelatin salads which were sold primarily to supermarkets and delicatessens in Oregon and Washington, with a limited number of sales to restaurants and hospitals. Additionally, we had the arrangement with Blue Bell, manufacturing and packaging potato-chip dip under their name.

As I saw it, the company also had two major liabilities. First, even though the dip sales had helped, our bottom line was still far too heavily dependent on sales during the summer months. If we were to grow, then we needed more products. And if we were to produce more products, we needed a bigger and more modern facility. More products and a more modern facility, however, required more cash, and our second major liability just happened to be the fact that our cash reserves were almost non-existent.

I knew that the dreams I had to grow the business couldn't become reality without money. I also knew that the most obvious place to find money was in a bank. I decided to write a business plan, with the intent of taking that plan to the bank to support a loan request. Never having written a business plan before, I was in need of some advice from someone with a lot more experience than I had—someone just like "Mac" McAllister.

Born in Portland, Oregon in the last decade of the nineteenth century, Mac had spent his entire career in the food business, working in turn for three giants of the industry—Armour, Kraft, and Borden's. Indeed, Mac had actually worked with J.R. Kraft, the founder of the company that bore his name. Mac and I first crossed paths during his years at Borden's, and he had retired from that company around the same time that I became president of Reser's. He was familiar with our business, and he had forgotten more about the food industry than I knew. I asked him if he would be willing to spend a few months helping me get my sea legs. Mac told me he had retired so he could go fishing whenever he wanted, and he had already determined that fishing whenever you wanted wasn't all that it was cracked up to be. He accepted my offer, and the "few months" for which he agreed to help out would end up stretching to twenty-five years.

It is hard to put into words the difference that Mac made, especially in those early years. My parents had not had the time or the interest to implement some basic business practices, like monthly financial statements and regular inventories. Mac immediately changed all that. He insisted that I have the most up-to-date financial information. He ensured that every bill to every customer was completely accurate. Every Friday, he personally directed a physical inventory of all finished goods, down to the last cup of gelatin salad. When we closed up shop for the week on Friday, Mac would promise me a complete financial report by the next Wednesday; more often than not, he would work all weekend and have the report for me on Monday. All this was especially important at first, as I was fighting for the financial survival of the business. Even today, nearly fifty years after he came to work for us, we are still using some of the forms and processes that Mac designed.

One of Mac's first assignments was to help me in devising the business plan that I would take to the banks. Convinced that we had developed a solid plan and could make a persuasive case that Reser's had a strong future and was a good investment, I put it in a classy-looking leather binder and headed off to the bank. They rejected my loan application. So I took the plan to another bank, where I received the same response. Eventually, I took the plan to every major bank in Oregon, receiving nothing but rejections. After every meeting and every rejection, I would ask myself "Why?" Was it the fact that they were unwilling to take a risk on a company with a president who was only twenty-five years old and fresh out of college? Was there something wrong with my business plan? Did they know something I didn't know about the future of the food business?

Mac and I sat down again, went over our numbers and projections, and concluded that our plan was a sound one. We decided that if we couldn't get the money we needed in Oregon, we might be able to get it three thousand miles away in New York City—by taking Reser's Fine Foods public through a stock offering.

I have long said that my diploma from Oregon State University was just the first of many I received in my career. Dealing with shrewd and seasoned Wall Street attorneys and stockbrokers was a remarkable learning experience that provided me with one more "diploma."

The current laws and regulations governing stock offerings are incredibly complex, but even in 1960 it was a mind-boggling maze of meetings, documents, and legal hoops. I had never set foot in New York City before I flew east for the first round of meetings on our prospectus, and I was more than a little intimidated at the beginning of the process. After a while, however, I found that I could hold my own. It dawned on me that what I lacked in age and experience, I could make up for with confidence and common sense.

One of the proudest days of my life was the day in December 1960 when the deal was finalized, all the documents signed, Reser's Fine Foods stock certificates were issued, and we were officially listed on what was then called the National Over-the-Counter Stock Exchange.

When the entire process was complete, we had an additional $400,000 in our bank account. This was a little less than I had hoped for, as I was surprised (not for the last time) by the amount that we had to pay to attorneys. It was enough, however, to purchase a new and substantially larger plant and headquarters for the company in Beaverton, Oregon, about twenty miles from our Cornelius facility. We moved into the 33,000-square-foot building in January 1961.

As I had hoped, the move to a larger facility increased our chances of economic survival. The additional space allowed us to improve operations through the purchase of a continuous potato cooker, which tripled our production, because we no longer had to cook potatoes in hundred-pound batches. The continuous potato cooker was designed by an engineer who worked for another food company and built in his garage. It was the first such machine in the industry, and it would serve us well for the next twenty years. I was very glad it didn't break down in those early years, because there was no way we could have afforded to repair it.

Tough Times Come and Go—Tough People Stay

As we moved into our new headquarters, my sister Lois looked first at the January date on the calendar—the slowest month of the year for salad sales—and then at our cavernous facility and wondered aloud, "What have we done?"

It was a good question. There were some who were skeptical of the purchase and who couldn't envision a future where we would actually need all of our new space. Our accountants bluntly told me that Reser's was a likely candidate for bankruptcy. I could tell from the balance sheet that there were reasons to be pessimistic, but I also knew that balance sheets don't tell the whole story, since they don't calculate perseverance, hard work, and a refusal to give up.

It would take four years of around-the-clock effort to reach a point where Reser's actually made a profit. And when profitability was finally achieved, I explained to our shareholders that instead of paying dividends, it made much more sense to retain the profit and invest every penny of it right back into the company.

During most of the 1960s, I went to work each day promising myself to work a little bit longer, to find one more new customer, or to convince one of our current customers that they needed to increase their order. The place to make all that happen wasn't behind a desk. Rather, it was on the road. I took one of our delivery trucks up and down Oregon's Willamette Valley, getting to know as many of our customers as possible. I wanted to hear their concerns and thank them for their loyalty in person. I wanted to see our displays to make sure they were presenting our products in the best possible manner. I wanted to get a feel for which products were selling best. Should that grocery store in Albany be buying more potato salad? Would sales increase if that deli in Salem had a more prominent display of our gelatin salads?

I was able to spend time on the road because I knew that operations back in Beaverton were in good hands. A business is no better than the people who work there, and I have been blessed for half a century to work with the hardest working, most loyal, and most creative people imaginable. I thank each member of our team—past and present—and pay tribute to them as I recall several individuals who refused to give up during those early lean times, and who made a priceless contribution to the Reser's story.

Lois Romaine: My sister, Lois Reser Romaine, managed the office during my early years as president, and she also served as secretary-treasurer of the business. One of the ways Lois watched over the company's money in a time when our cash flow was very tight was to make sure we weren't paying our bills one minute earlier than necessary. Lois had a way with words, and she totally charmed our suppliers, convincing them to continue to sell to us, even though we might not yet have paid our previous bill. She promised them we would pay as soon as possible, and it was a promise we always kept. Lois continued to work as a liaison to some of our most important customers until cancer forced her to retire. She passed away in 2009, and she is greatly missed.

"Gramps": He was my mother's father, and everyone in the business knew him simply as "Gramps." After going broke in the Depression, Gramps had operated a small Kansas grocery store for a time, and he had a knack for the food business. He moved to Oregon in the mid-1950s, a few years after my family arrived, and was one of the original members of the crew who made and packaged my mother's potato salad.

It was Gramps who loaned me the money to buy my father's share of the business in 1960, and he never wanted to be far from the action. He continued to help in product preparation and, as the business grew, took charge of our warehouse, where he was renowned for his meticulous records of shipments and deliveries. Gramps could have filled almost any job in the business, and he could smell a problem almost before it began, letting me know immediately if something wasn't right. He also served unofficially as a one-man education department, training countless Reser's employees. He seemed to know when I was struggling with a decision, and he would quietly weigh in with his opinion, leaving no doubt that he was always in favor of investments and actions that would grow the business.

One of Gramps' legacies is my collection of large piggy banks, which are all filled to the brim with pennies. "Watch the pennies and the dollars will take care of themselves," was a piece of advice Gramps often repeated, and for nearly half a century one of the first things I do when I come home after work is to place every penny I've received during the day into one of those banks. I don't know how many thousands of pennies are in those banks, or just what I'm going to do with them eventually, but I suspect that one day they will all be given to charity in memory of Gramps.

My kids would tell you that Gramps was also a very special great-grandfather. He joined us for dinner every Sunday, and his pockets were always full of gum and candy. Gramps worked until the day before he died, and many of our long-time employees still take time to tell me how much they loved him.

Darrell Vandehey: Having three sisters was great, but I confess there was a time or two when I was growing up when I wished that I had a brother. That wish came true when my family moved from our cabin to the farmhouse in Cornelius. Not only did we have a larger kitchen, which allowed my parents to increase production of potato salad, but we also had next-door neighbors—the Vandehey family. Darrell Vandehey and I have been best friends from almost the day we met. Within a few weeks, we had constructed a crude communications device out of old hand-cranked phones and wire. We ran the wire from my bedroom down a tree, over some hay bales, where it connected to a barbed wire fence. The barbed wire then served as the connecting wire for the mile or so distance to the driveway at Darrell's house. We then connected some more wire from the end of the fence up another tree, and into Darrell's bedroom. Believe it or not, on a clear night, we could talk back and forth just like we were standing next to each other. A little rain, however, would cause static that made our conversation hard to understand.

Darrell's mother, Ida, was one of the first employees of Mrs. Reser's Salads, and before long Darrell was also working for my parents. Once we turned sixteen, Darrell and I took on delivery duties, loading freshly made potato, macaroni, and gelatin salads into the back seat of my parents' Nash automobile, covering them with dry ice and a blanket, and heading down the road.

Darrell also joined me during spring break of my sophomore year in high school in an ill-fated attempt to pick up some extra money by working as "tree fallers" on a small logging project my father had organized. Our job was to help cut down about three hundred trees which were to be used as material for telephone poles. We were to be paid one dollar for each tree and were very excited about the prospect of making three hundred dollars, which was big money back then. Our dreams of wealth were quickly popped, and my logging career ended almost before it began, when the very first tree we cut down didn't fall in the direction we intended, and instead landed squarely on a brand new Ford that belonged to another worker involved in the project!

Darrell would go on to graduate from OSU in 1960 with a degree in food technology, which he quickly put to use by joining Reser's full time. His early assignments included selling and delivering salads to stores on the Oregon coast. In 1962 he became Vice President of

Production, a position he held until 2000, when he tried to retire. This attempt at retirement failed—most every morning he comes to the office to make sure everything is going smoothly.

There were a few additional titles that Darrell should have held over the years but didn't. One is "chief mechanic and electrician"—there isn't a piece of machinery or equipment that Darrell doesn't know or can't fix. Since nothing drags production to a halt faster then broken machinery, Darrell spent most of his career on call twenty-four hours a day, seven days a week. The other title is "Assistant Chief Taster"—Darrell has always enjoyed sampling products and offering his suggestions for improvement. As a member of the board of directors for nearly half a century, Darrell has been involved in almost every major business decision in the history of Reser's, and I can't imagine the last fifty years without him.

The Best Way To Predict the Future Is To Create It

If the key to succeeding in real estate is location, location, location, the key to succeeding in the food business is innovation, innovation, innovation. The one constant in the food business—in fact, in most businesses—is change. The tastes of consumers are always evolving, and businesses must evolve with them if they hope to survive. I knew from my first day as president that if the only products we continued to make were potato, macaroni, and gelatin salads, then we wouldn't be around much longer.

Our first ventures into new products were ones with the specific purpose of taking the seasonality out of our business, and increasing sales beyond the summer months. We began to produce caramel apples for the Halloween season, and "Tom and Jerry" and hot buttered rum mixes for the holiday months. To paraphrase an old saying, "a caramel apple a day helped keep bankruptcy away," as we sold a hundred thousand cases of caramel apples that first autumn. With 24 to the case, that totaled out to 2.4 million apples. At a dime an apple, that was an important $240,000 increase in our annual sales.

By the way, while caramel apples taste great, they are a mess to make—especially when you're making 2.4 million of them. We are no longer in the caramel apple business, but there are long-time Reser employees who tell me they still remember how difficult it was to remove sticky caramel from their work clothes.

The success of the caramel apples encouraged me to keep thinking of ideas for new products. To be sure, not every idea I have had over the years was a winning one. For example, since sour cream-based dips were popular for potato chips, I thought that a similar product might work on baked potatoes and other cooked vegetables. We developed, produced, and marketed a potato and veg-etable topping called "Hi-Hat." While some consumers took to the product, most decided that they would rather stick to putting plain sour cream on their baked potato.

Another product that didn't live up to my initial expectations developed out of Reser family breakfasts. Pat had some cookie cutters in the shape of circus animals, which she used to mold pancakes. Our kids loved biting the heads off of giraffe- or elephant-shaped pancakes. It occurred to me that they would also like to bite off the heads of hamburger patties shaped like giraffes or elephants. It wasn't long before we produced and marketed "Jungle Patties"—frozen meat patties in the shape of jungle animals. I suppose we should have subjected the patties to more rigorous product testing, because we discovered too late that the patties would "lose their identity" as they cooked in the skillet, becoming shapeless blobs that all looked exactly the same.

Then there was chili hot-dog sauce. Americans buy millions of packages of hot dogs each year, and I figured that if just ten percent of those buying hot dogs also bought our sauce—to turn their hot dog into a "chili dog"—then we had a sure-fire winner. Despite running almost every promotion I could think of, including having grocery stores give away the sauce with purchase of a package of hot dogs, the product never took off.

There are more than a few people—including Pat—who won't let me forget "Steak in a Box." Believe me, it tasted better than it sounds. The package contained four high-quality lean, thick steaks at a great price, ready to throw on the barbecue or in the skillet. We introduced the product into the market and initially achieved some encouraging sales numbers. I thought we could increase those numbers through a television commercial featuring Jim Bosley, who was a very popular weather forecaster on a local Portland television station. Traditionally, we had not relied on television ads, and since I wasn't an advertising expert, I turned the writing and production process over to Bosley. When it came time to tape the commercial, I watched from the sidelines as Bosley demonstrated for an attractive blonde woman just how easy it was and what a bargain it was to cook great steaks for your family. He ended the ad by looking at the camera and proclaiming with a smile on his face, "Reser's Steak in a Box—so easy to make, even a blonde can do it." Now, this was back in the early 1980s, when it seemed like everyone had a so-called "dumb blonde" joke; the camera crew laughed at Bosley's line and assured me it was a great commercial. I should have known better. The morning after it ran on air for the first time, our telephones were overwhelmed with calls from women who thought the ad was insulting. And when Pat happened to catch the commercial, she made it very clear exactly what she thought of it. I quickly ordered the commercial removed from broadcast, but the sales—or lack of them—in the following months suggested that countless blondes—and brunettes and redheads—had already resolved never to buy "Steak in a Box."

Throughout the years, I have told Reser's employees the stories of my ideas that didn't pan out, and I've made the point that ideas that don't succeed are nothing to be ashamed of. My goal has been to create and maintain a work environment that encourages managers and employees to be creative. I like to say that we are a company of dreamers. We throw a lot of spaghetti at the wall and see what sticks. We might just have one winner out of fifty ideas, but there is excitement in trying something new. And while potato salad remains Reser's best seller, it has been new products and new ideas that have propelled us to our position as an industry leader.

In 1963, for example, we became aware of steady growth in the Hispanic population in Oregon. We responded by becoming the first Northwest company to produce fresh tortillas, even though many of our customers had never heard of tacos or burritos, and certainly didn't know how to prepare them. We helped to alleviate that problem by holding demonstrations in grocery stores teaching customers the fine art of taco making. As the popularity of Mexican food continued to grow over the years, so did the number of products we offered. In 2002, we launched "Baja Café," a line of tortillas, salsas, burritos, tacquitos, tamales, flautas, and other Mexican foods. Some forty-four years after we entered the Mexican food market, we now make well over five million tortillas each day.

I happen to believe that Reser's salsa, which we began to produce in the early 1980s, is the best on the market—and a few years back I discovered that one of America's most legendary movie stars agrees with me. Our sales office received a call from a gentleman at Warner Brothers Studios in Hollywood, who identified himself as the assistant to Clint Eastwood. He said that Mr. Eastwood wanted to know if we were the company that produced "the salsa with the yellow lid." The very next day, Patty McCormack and Rachel Grant, our sales representatives in southern California, were on the way to Mr. Eastwood's office with a special salsa delivery. He personally met our representatives and said that he had first become acquainted with our salsa in Idaho, and thought it was the best on the market. You can bet that when I learned all of this, Clint had really "made my day."

Keep Your Eye on the Horizon, Not Just the Bottom Line

By the early 1970s, I was feeling increasingly optimistic about the future of the company. We had recently purchased Sausage Kitchen, a Milwaukie, Oregon, business that processed pepperoni and a variety of sausage products. The purchase allowed us to further diversify our product line and helped raise our annual sales to $13 million. But in 1973 and 1974, a series of circumstances threatened the viability of Reser's, reminding me that the line between business success and failure is a small one—and something that is not always within your control.

The troubles began with a period of rapid inflation that substantially raised the price of meat, potatoes, mayonnaise, and other principal ingredients used by the company. The price of sugar doubled in just two months. In addition, an oil shortage led to a skyrocketing increase in the price of gasoline, dramatically increasing our transportation and delivery costs. The end result of these increases was that we hit a series of months where the company was hemorrhaging money.

Others in the food industry were experiencing the same difficulties. I watched as some of our competitors cut costs by substituting ingredients that were lower in price—and in quality. Some in our company who were looking at the bottom line urged me to follow suit. I refused to do it. My belief was that while we would save money by cutting costs, we would lose something that you could never put a price on—the trust of our customers. I decided that we would hunker down, work at becoming more efficient, and weather the tough times the best we could—but that we would not take any actions that would diminish the quality of our products. Throughout the years, I have always tried to remember that while the numbers on our bottom line are obviously very important, a good leader always keeps his eyes on the horizon, weighing and understanding the long-term implications of each decision.

Know What You Don't Know

I have encountered more than a few executives in the food industry who brag about having total knowledge and control of every aspect of their business. My philosophy is different. I don't know everything. But I hire great people who know what I don't.

Take the transportation of Reser's products, for example. The rules and regulations governing interstate trucking of goods are an incredibly arcane and confusing maze of paperwork. This was especially true in the 1970s, before the federal government deregulated the trucking industry. It was very apparent to me that if I wanted to become an expert in transportation issues, then I wouldn't have much time to do anything else.

Instead, what made sense to me was to hire someone who would become an expert in those issues, and to let that individual do their job. I gave that responsibility to Gayle Bergstrom, telling her that I only had two expectations: First, customer service was our top priority, and I never wanted to hear from a customer that a delivery had not arrived on time. Second, Reser's should never receive a fine from the federal or state government transportation agencies governing interstate trucking. The steps she took to meet those expectations were entirely up to her, because I would not be looking over her shoulder as a micro-manager. Along with giving your employees a job and a salary, you need to give them your trust. I trusted Gayle, and she did her job: Reser's never has been fined for a transportation violation, and while a truck or two might have been a few minutes late, our customers still rave about our commitment to on-time delivery.

Don't Manage by Stereotypes

Gayle's story also highlights another principle of my management style: if a manager places limits on employees because of their gender or age, then the manager is making a foolish mistake.

Women do the vast majority of grocery shopping, and comprise the majority of customers for the food industry. Despite that, the executive ranks of the food industry in the 1960s, '70s and '80s remained overwhelmingly male. Given that there would have been no Reser's Fine Foods without my mother's ingenuity and perseverance, I never understood the reluctance of many food industry executives to promote women to management levels. My sole test for managers is whether or not they can do the job, and the fact that interstate trucking was one of the most male-dominated businesses did not stop me from hiring Gayle.

While many companies still enforce mandatory retirement ages, Reser's does not. As I write this book, I am seventy-four years young and continue to serve as CEO and Chairman of the Board. I still enjoy coming to work and believe that I am making an important contribution. It would be hypocritical of me to decree that just because someone is sixty-five or seventy years old, then they are automatically disqualified from continuing to make their own contribution. If they are performing the duties of their job and want to keep working, then we are honored to benefit from their experience.

All Work and No Play Is a Lousy Recipe

One of the first employees my parents hired was an incredible woman named Nellie Mae Jacques, who would eventually work for the business for twenty-two years.

No one was more reliable or dependable than Nellie, and no one loved coming to work more than she did. Nellie passed away a few years ago, but when she was over ninety years old, she gave an interview in which she recalled the early years of her job, saying: "I put in a lot of hours and I didn't mind it at all because we were all good friends. It was just a fun place to work." She went on to describe how my parents would break up the monotony by having contests to see who could peel the most potatoes, with the losers chipping in to buy beer for the winners.

The example set by my mother and father has stayed with me throughout my life. No matter how large we have grown, or how many employees are on our payroll, I have always insisted on making each of our facilities a fun and enjoyable place to come to work each day. It wouldn't be Reser's without our annual summer picnic, Halloween party, and December holiday party. And it certainly wouldn't be Reser's without the good-natured ribbing that goes on in the week leading up to the annual "Civil War" football game between Oregon State University and the University of Oregon. Paul Leavy, our current Chief Financial Officer, is a proud University of Oregon graduate, and one year he came to work the day before the Civil War game to discover that his office had been mysteriously painted orange and black—the team colors of the Beavers.

Indeed, as I look back on my life, the memories that mean the most are not memories of yet another sales meeting; rather, they are memories of laughing with family, friends, and co-workers. Pat and I still shake our heads recalling one July 4th party we hosted for a hundred and fifty or so guests. Pat had decided on a Hawaiian theme, and the main course was to be a spit-roasted pig. When the morning of the party arrived, we drove to a warehouse to pick up the star of the show—the freshly butchered pig. Much to our surprise, however, we discovered that instead of being refrigerated, the carcass had been placed in a freezer, and it was now hard as a rock. We spent the rest of the day running hot water on the inside and outside of the pig, warming it with hair dryers, even taking a blowtorch to it, before it had finally thawed enough to take its place of honor on the spit. Dinner was served three hours late that night, but our guests showed a great deal of patience and good humor.

I also remember a night of much laughter while attending a food distributors convention and exposition in Dallas, Texas. As Pat and I and the other convention attendees returned to our hotel after a day of meetings and banquets, we couldn't help but notice a baby grand piano in the mezzanine. Pat is a gifted pianist, and before you could say "karaoke," a group of us had maneuvered the piano into a hotel freight elevator and taken it up to the floor where we were staying. We couldn't fit it through the door to our room, so we set it up in the hall, where Pat began playing, and about a hundred of us began singing. The hotel security guards said the party would have to break up if any guest complained, so we went door to door on our floor, inviting everyone to join in the fun.

It wasn't until two in the morning that we delivered the piano—no worse for wear—back to the mezzanine.

Those who attended a recent Refrigerated Foods Association gathering are probably still talking about the unusual race I engaged in with my friend and fellow longtime refrigerated-food executive Vinny Gruppuso. A number of back surgeries have forced me to rely upon a motorized scooter to get around, and Vinny, the founder of Kozy Shack, a refrigerated pudding and dessert manufacturer based in Hicksville, New York, is in a similar condition. A lighthearted quip by Pat that the two of us should race each other quickly snowballed into the banquet tables being pushed aside, a race course set up, and wagers made—with the winner donating the proceeds to charity. I don't want to brag by revealing who won, but they don't call me "Leadfoot Al" for nothing, and more than $5,000 was soon on its way to one of my favorite non-profit organizations.

Find People with Passion

I've interviewed countless job applicants over the years, looked at countless resumes, and have a good track record of hiring great people. If there is one quality I look for in prospective employees it is passion. You can't teach passion or learn passion, but it is passion that makes work more than a job.

If you want to be an accountant, then you need to have a passion for accounting. If you dream of a career as a lawyer, then you need a passion for the law. I have a passion for the food business, and I want to be surrounded by people who think it is a fascinating, challenging, and rewarding field of work.

One sign of passion is that you care about more than just the place you work—you care about your entire industry. Some of the most rewarding moments of my career occurred when I met with executives from other refrigerated-food companies to discuss common problems and share ideas. In 1980, Reser's was one of the twelve founding members of the Salad Manufacturers Association. Since then, the organization has changed its name to the Refrigerated Foods Association, seen membership swell to over 120 companies, and has served as a valuable clearinghouse for information on technical, regulatory, and safety issues. I am proud to report that Mark and I are one of the few father-and-son teams to have each served a term as president of the RFA.

FIVE

t goes without saying that Reser's is in the food business. But I surprise folks when I tell them that we are actually in the people business, as well. Watching my parents' friends and neighbors working in our Cornelius kitchen taught me at an early age how important it is to treat employees with respect—to treat them like family. As Reser's grew through the 1960s and 1970s, and we expanded from a handful of employees to hundreds of employees, I worked to keep this lesson in mind. My job was not just to sit behind a desk or meet only with our biggest customers. My job was also to walk through every production line, to visit with and get to know every employee.

My philosophy was to treat our customers with the same respect I gave to our employees. Letters and phone calls were to be answered quickly and courteously. Complaints were to be handled seriously, and, if necessary, corrections made quickly. You don't just get customers, you build relationships and make friends. If you just get customers, you can lose them. If you build relationships, you keep friends.

If I ever needed any validation of the importance of treating employees and customers with respect, it came in the early 1980s, when our success and growth made us the target of a corporate takeover.

The first round of what would become a several-years-long struggle began when I received word from the United States Securities and Exchange Commission that an individual had purchased ten percent of the shares of Reser's stock, and was in the process of buying more. I made a few phone calls and discovered that the person behind the purchases was Atlee Kohl. Kohl was a prominent and successful investor who specialized in building a large business by taking over a number of small businesses in the same industry. Kohl had set his sights on the food industry, and his investment firm had already purchased four small food companies with annual sales in the $10- to $50-million range. His goal was to obtain a controlling interest in another four to six similar companies—Reser's included.

I flew to Texas to meet with Kohl and to confirm his intentions. He was very straightforward in telling me that he was indeed putting together a consortium of food companies and would do whatever it took to buy the fifty-one percent of our stock that would ensure Reser's was part of his empire. He also made it clear to me that if I wanted to sell him my stock, he would pay me a price that would make me a very rich man. My decision to refuse his offer and to fight for my company was not a difficult one to make. I loved what I was doing and I loved the company. I had spent over two decades working to ensure that the business would survive and grow. I wanted to keep on doing just that for many more years to come.

Kohl was a shrewd and experienced businessman who knew how to play hardball. In an attempt to reach our stockholders, most of whom lived in the Pacific Northwest, Kohl purchased full-page newspaper ads in regional newspapers offering top dollar for shares in Reser's. He also spoke to the media, offering a highly unflattering analysis of my leadership of Reser's. Within a number of months, Kohl held forty-four percent of our stock, and outside observers thought it likely that he would soon get the remaining amount he needed to win majority control.

I knew that if it came down to money, then Kohl would win. He had access to financial resources that would allow him to offer stockholders more than I could offer them. But while I couldn't match Kohl in terms of cash, I outdid him when it came to reputation and relationships. Many of the small shareholders that he had not yet approached were Reser's customers or Reser's employees, and as I met with each of them, I discovered that they were proud of what Reser's had accomplished over the years. They were proud that we were a homegrown business. They were proud of our reputation for service and quality. They were proud of our support of community organizations. Our employees were grateful for the family atmosphere, for the respect they were given, and for the fact that their opinions, suggestions, and creativity were encouraged.

I was gratified beyond measure that shareholders and employees saw me not just as CEO of a company, but as their friend. As a result, they were sympathetic to my request that they sell their shares to me on favorable two- and three-year terms, or that they give me right of first refusal to purchase their stock. Eventually, I was able to call Kohl and tell him that I had secured the votes of a sufficient number of shareholders to prevent him from ever reaching majority control.

Kohl and I both knew that although his effort had failed, Reser's would remain a likely target for the other takeover artists who were so prevalent on Wall Street in the 1980s. We both knew that the only way for me to avoid another takeover attempt was to return the company to private ownership. Kohl called me on Christmas Eve 1986 with an offer. He had purchased his shares at prices ranging from a low of 35 to 40 cents a share to a high of four dollars a share, and told me he would be happy to sell me all his stock for fourteen dollars a share. He added that if I was to accept his offer, then he wanted the cash by New Year's Eve. Anticipating what Kohl had up his sleeve, I had already initiated the process of lining up the loan necessary for me to meet his demands. Reser's Fine Foods was again a family owned business—although one that now had a huge new 1.65-million-dollar debt.

There Are Risks You Can't Afford To Take, and There Are Risks You Can't Afford Not To Take

With the battle for control of the company won, my management team and I could concentrate on answering a question that demanded a response. Our annual sales had grown from $300,000 when I became president in 1960 to nearly $40 million some twenty-five years later. It was clear that Reser's was on solid ground. The question that needed answering, however, was whether or not the status quo was good enough. Were we happy with our position as a strong regional company with almost all our customers and sales in the western United States? Or could we be something more? Did we have what it takes to become a larger company with additional products and national processing and distribution capabilities? It was a decision that involved a good deal of risk.

Indeed, every decision made by a business owner involves some degree of risk, as there is never a complete guarantee as to how a decision will turn out. Taking risks paralyzes some but it empowers others. I confess that I enjoy risk. My family and friends will unanimously agree with that analysis, as most of them have joined me over the years on an occasional quick trip to Las Vegas or Reno, Nevada. The fact is, there's a great deal in common between the casino table and the business table. Whether it's rolling dice or deciding whether or not to start a new product line, you must remain calm and focused. You need to understand the odds, and be ready for the consequences—good and bad—of your decision.

I have made countless decisions over the years. Some involved more risk than I was willing to take. With others, I concluded that I couldn't afford not to take the risk, and that's exactly what I concluded on the question of taking Reser's to the next level. I knew it would take lots of money, hard work, and a little bit of luck to expand successfully in the Midwestern, Southern, and Eastern markets. I also knew that since the company was a privately held family business, the risk was much more personal. I would be risking my own reserves and capital. If I needed outside financing, I would sign for the money personally. If my decision to expand nationally proved to be a bad one, I would bear all of the loss. Still, the amount of risk was secondary to my determination to make our expansion successful.

The years after the company returned to private ownership were to be some of the busiest of my career. I spent countless hours on airplanes, as I joined my sales managers in flying around the country to introduce Reser's to companies who had not previously purchased our products, and to convince current customers to increase their orders.

I especially remember one meeting in Little Rock, Arkansas, with managers from Safeway. While the Safeway stores in Oregon and the West had remained loyal customers of Reser's since the early 1950s, I was hoping to convince Safeway managers in the Midwest and the South that they should also do business with us. Little Rock, home to a divisional headquarters of Safeway, was one of our first stops, and our sales manager Ron Leeper and I arrived at headquarters in plenty of time to set up a "tasting table" featuring samples of a variety of our salads. As we were stirring and garnishing the salads to make sure they looked just right, a casually dressed gentleman walked in, grabbed some spoons, and began to taste some of the salads. Assuming he was a mid-level employee, I told him he was welcome to taste a few samples, but that we were preparing for a tasting session with all the "big wheels" of the company, so he would need to depart in a few minutes. He said he understood how important it was to impress the "big wheels" and immediately left the room. He returned about three-quarters of the way through our formal tasting session, and the other executives immediately moved him to the front of the tasting line, and introduced him to me as the division manager—in other words, he was the biggest wheel in Little Rock.

As he came over to shake my hand, I'm sure I turned as red as the paprika on our potato salad. Thankfully, as well as being a big wheel, he had a sense of humor, and he assured me that I had not blown our opportunity to make a sale. In fact, he would eventually rise through the ranks to become a top executive at Safeway corporate headquarters, and each time I met with him, he would good-naturedly ask me if he was a big enough wheel.

Increasing sales was one part of our growth strategy. Acquiring food manufacturing companies with complementary product lines or food distribution companies in areas new to us was another. Over the course of the past twenty years, the businesses we have purchased include Salad Host in Corona, California; Hawaiian Eateries

Salads in Honolulu, Hawaii; Mrs. Weaver's Salads in Memphis, Tennessee; Manor Hill Foods in Baltimore, Maryland; Sidari's Italian Foods in Cleveland, Ohio; Bellissima Italia in Beaverton, Oregon; La Siesta Foods in Topeka, Kansas; Don Pancho Authentic Mexican Foods in Salem, Oregon; Mrs. Giles Country Kitchens in Lynchburg, Virginia; Mrs. Kinser's Salads in Knoxville, Tennessee; Tortillas San Antonio in Nashville, North Carolina; and Lynn Wilson Foods in Salt Lake City, Utah.

Buying privately held businesses is actually a fairly easy and quick process. Once we identified a company with a product or a territory that made strategic and economic sense, I would meet with their executives to see if they were interested in selling. Having been the subject of an attempted hostile takeover, I wanted no part in acquiring a business that didn't want to be acquired. Most of the businesses we purchased were very much like Reser's—family-owned operations that began very small and slowly achieved growth and success.

The hard work of buying a business actually occurs after the deal is done. Following each purchase, we devoted a great deal of time to meeting with our new employees and introducing them to the culture and values of Reser's.

Big Business Doesn't Mean Big Bureaucracy

Back when our annual sales were only $300,000, I had a policy that any employee could walk into my office and share their thoughts and suggestions. And when it came time to reach an important decision, I would gather all the necessary people in a room, and we would walk out with a decision.

I believe that one of the reasons our annual sales are now approaching $700 million is that fact that those policies have remained the same throughout the decades. Reser's is a company where bureaucracy and red tape are kept at an absolute minimum. Employees still don't need to call and make an appointment to see me, and where some of our competitors have six to eight months of meetings before a final decision is made concerning a new product, we take six to eight days.

Being nimble and flexible has allowed us to react quickly to new market trends and to continue to lead the industry in innovation. In the early 1990s, for example, we looked again at the product that began the whole Reser's story—the potato. In order to keep our Topeka, Kansas, salad plant operating at full capacity beyond the summer months, we had begun producing fresh refrigerated hash-brown potatoes for customers in the food-service industry. Almost before we knew it, we were producing six million pounds annually.

Around the same time, Pat and I and several members of my management team traveled to Europe for an international food show. I was impressed by the number of exhibits at the show that featured different styles of refrigerated potatoes, which were very popular in England, Germany, Holland, and other European countries.

European consumers could go to their local grocery store and find fresh refrigerated potatoes cut in every size and shape, including potato "rounds" that ranged from marble-size to golf ball-size. After returning from Europe, I called our top managers together one weekend to discuss what we had learned, and where we saw the American potato market moving in the future. Before the meeting was over, we had reached a decision to build a new state-of-the-art facility dedicated to refrigerated potatoes. We created a new line of "Potato Express" products which featured sliced, diced, and mashed potatoes that were ready for the dinner table after, on average, four minutes in the skillet, oven, or microwave. We now produce and deliver nearly a hundred million pounds of refrigerated potato products annually.

The Power of "See Me"

It is probably safe to say that every executive or manager at Reser's has received the same memo from me at one time or another. The memo consists of three short words—"See me, Al."

The "see me" memo is attached to a report that the manager has prepared and sent to my office. I read every report very carefully, and I usually have a question or two; or I see something that impresses me, intrigues me, or concerns me. So I write a quick "see me" memo on the report and send it back to where it came from.

Why don't I write my reaction on the report? First, I vastly prefer face-to-face meetings over written reports. And second, I have discovered that when someone receives my "see me" memo, they immediately engage in some additional thinking, invariably wondering what part of their report caught my attention. They read their report again, double check the numbers, reconsider or confirm their recommendations, and often come to my office with a new creative or innovative proposal.

The bottom line for executives is that if you want to hear some brains clicking into overdrive, just remember the power of "see me."

The Four Cornerstones of Reser's

Ask a hundred Reser's employees which of our products they like best and you'll likely get a hundred different answers. But ask about the principles which have always been at the core of our business and you are likely to hear the same four words again and again: Service. Consistency. Safety. Value.

Service: My mother's determination that her salads would be delivered fresh to customers every Sunday, even if it meant working twenty-four hours straight on Saturday, has always served as a reminder to me of the critical importance of customer service. My philosophy—in good times and bad—has always been that customers are the reason we are here and they are number one. For example, if a delivery truck is just pulling out of the driveway and there's two inches of space on it and a customer wants another case of potato salad, then that product is going on the truck. I take great pride in the fact that there are customers who have been with us for four and five decades, and it's our commitment to customer service that will ensure they are with us forever.

Safety: An absolute necessity for success in the food business is the trust of the retailers who sell your products and the consumers who buy them. The only way to win that trust is a complete and total commitment to food safety. As was seen in the peanut industry in 2009, any deviation from that commitment can endanger the health of the public, and lead to newspaper headlines, lawsuits, and financial ruin.

At Reser's, our commitment to food safety can be seen in the fact that we don't just meet government-mandated safety requirements, we go beyond them. You can see the emphasis we place on safety by following a potato as it enters our plant to eventually become part of our potato salad:

First, before processing starts each day, Quality Assurance personnel conduct pre-operation inspections. Along with a visual check of all production areas, QA personnel take swabs of all equipment, floors, drains, walls and other processing areas surfaces for microbiological testing. Once they are satisfied, machinery can be reassembled and production can begin.

Potatoes are delivered to the processing room via an enclosed pipe that runs along the plant's roof and funnels down through a steam peeler, which heats and peels batches of potatoes. Potatoes leaving the peeler move next to a scrubber, where circular rotating brushes remove remaining scraps of peel. Afterwards, potatoes are quickly diced into half-inch cubes, and are inspected by a computerized camera. Potatoes that don't meet our high standards are rejected by laser technology. Potatoes that "make the cut" are moved to an ambient steam tunnel cooker, which heats the potatoes to more than two hundred degrees Fahrenheit. To firm up starches within the potatoes and to ensure the potato segments can withstand processing, they are next run through a continuous pre-cooler and cooler that reduces their temperature first to sixty degrees and then to below forty degrees. Potatoes exit the cooler after fifteen to twenty minutes and are transferred to stainless totes. The totes are wheeled into a central storage cooler for the three-hour period that is required to complete the starch-setting process.

Computer-controlled delivery systems transfer wet ingredients such as mayonnaise, mustard, celery, relish, and onions to the ribbon mixer, where they are blended in eight- to twelve-hundred-pound batches. By this point, the totes of potatoes have been placed in the processing room, and poured into the mixer. A forty-five-second blending sequence then thoroughly mixes the ingredients without damaging the potatoes. During the processing, QA team members continually take samples, double checking them for overall quality. After the potato salad is packaged in containers, it is stored in refrigerated areas at below 38 degrees, where it is loaded and shipped via our fleet of refrigerated trucks to our customers.

The German leader Otto von Bismarck once said that it's better not to see "laws or sausages" being made. The bottom line is that anyone who watched potato salad or any other of our products being made would walk away secure in the knowledge that food safety is more than just a goal, it's a way of life at Reser's.

Consistency: Along with being a provider of food, I'm also a consumer of food. And nothing bothers me more than eating at a restaurant or buying a product where the quality varies from day to day. It has often been observed that one of the key reasons behind the success of McDonald's is that customers know the hamburger and french fries they purchase today will taste exactly like the ones they purchased yesterday.

Reser's achieves consistent high quality through a number of steps. First, we only buy the best and freshest ingredients available. Our Quality Assurance department has a strict set of guidelines which must be met by each of our vendors. We are constantly consulting with farmers to make sure that their potatoes, tomatoes, celery, and other crops are as good as they can be. Second, we have standardized recipes and mixing procedures that mean no guessing is done during the manufacturing process. Finally, once our product is manufactured, we deliver it to our customers as quickly as possible.

Value: Reser's is all about families. We are a family business, and our products are ones that bring families together at meals. We also understand that families have budgets, and that our mission is to provide families with good food at a fair price.

Keeping costs low so that prices can stay low is a constant battle for any business. Even though my career as an accountant lasted just two weeks, I have long believed that my accounting education probably did me more long-term good than anything else I could have studied. During the lean times, my knowledge of accounting helped me understand our dire economic circumstances, and what we needed to do to survive. As we grew over the years, my accounting education also gave me an ability to pencil out the costs and benefits of a variety of expansions and purchases. So my advice to anyone who is planning a career in business is to have a solid understanding of accounting principles.

Speaking of accounting, I recall an occasion back in the early 1960s when Reser's was undergoing our annual audit by our accounting firm. The young accountant assigned to the audit was a gentleman by the name of Phil Knight. Like me, Knight would also leave the accounting field for bigger dreams. Nike, the company he founded, has its corporate headquarters literally across the street from ours. I often joke that Nike shoes cost much more per ounce than our salads!

SIX

he goals of a family business are not mysterious. You want your business to be profitable, provide a good standard of living for your family members, and appreciate in value. You also want all members of the family to be happy. The trick is to accomplish the first goal without endangering the second, because there is always the very real concern that business pressures will cause tension, jealousy, or resentments that could split the family apart. It takes careful work to prevent that from happening, and the statistics suggest that the careful work does not always succeed.

There are somewhere around twenty million "family businesses" in the United States. Of these, it is estimated that about thirty-five percent will successfully pass to the second generation, twelve percent will continue to the third generation, and only two percent will continue to the fourth generation. That's a ninety-eight-percent dropout rate from the first generation to the fourth generation.

2008 was a banner year at Reser's, as Nikki, the daughter of my son Marty and his wife, Jane, began work in the human resources department at our Beaverton headquarters, becoming the first member of the fourth generation to join the family business.

How has Reser's beaten the odds? I can answer that question in one simple word: Pat. She has been and continues to be a remarkable wife, mother, and grandmother. I became president of Reser's just a few months after the birth of our son, Marty, in 1960. Ten years later, our daughter, Mindy, would join our family as our fifth and final child. In between, we welcomed Michael in 1961, Mark in 1965, and Michelle in 1967. While I was at the office or on the road far too much, it was Pat who attended to the far more important job of being a parent, attending every school sporting event, concert, and conference. And until Mark's birth, it was Pat who smoothly juggled parenting with her job as a public school teacher, thereby contributing to the family's income during a time when Reser's Fine Foods was basically a break-even proposition. I am also very proud that when the children were grown, Pat returned to school and earned her Masters Degree in Special Education.

Pat and the kids were extremely patient with me over the years, and I tried to replace quantity of time with quality, treasuring weekend breakfasts where I would serve as the chef. I suppose some may have regarded me as a "workaholic," as I put in hour after hour in the office and on the road. Even when I wasn't "on the clock," I still couldn't keep my mind off the business. No matter where we traveled on family vacations, I always seemed to find my way to a local supermarket, so I could check out new ideas in products and packaging and make sure all displays of Reser's products were clean and attractive.

Pat and I introduced the kids to the family business by taking them to the office and plant on Saturdays. They learned always to look for the Reser's displays in supermarkets, and to call me if they thought something was wrong. They also served as unofficial "taste testers" for Reser's, as I brought samples from new recipes home for them to try. Five "thumbs up" from the Reser kids meant that we had a winner.

As my children grew up and entered high school and college, they all worked at the business. But, instead of starting in the executive suite, they all began working in production, sanitation, or preparation. Every one of them spent time washing our delivery trucks. We wanted them to learn every job, and to instill in them an understanding that just because they were Resers, they were no different from any other employee. We wanted them to know that because their name was Reser, they needed to be more responsible and more caring as they worked to earn the respect of their co-workers. We cautioned them that their mistakes would loom larger and their successes diminished, and they needed to understand that and learn from those experiences.

Finally, as they moved into the company full-time following college, we made it clear that their jobs were not an entitlement. Rather, they were earned, and depended upon their strengths and interests. Mark, now Reser's president, joined the company in 1987 as a route salesman. After earning "Salesman of the Year" honors, he took on operations responsibilities at our plants in

Corona, California, and Topeka, Kansas, before returning to headquarters in Beaverton. Mike's strengths and interests are in customer service, where he plays a major role in nurturing customers and meeting their needs as vice president of logistics. Marty started as a route salesman right out of college, and proved himself a natural in the sales business, as he worked his way up to sales supervisor to district manager to vice president of retail sales, setting new sales records every step of the way. Marty recently set up his own brokerage firm, handling some key Reser accounts. Michelle worked in our marketing department for several years after receiving her Masters degree at OSU, and still helps manage strategic projects, while tending to more important duties as a wife, mother, and community volunteer. Mindy, who came home from college nearly every weekend to earn some money washing our delivery trucks, has now earned the envy of her brothers and sister by building and operating a luxury seaside health spa near Puerto Vallarta, Mexico.

While the business prevented me from spending as much time as I would have liked with my children, it did bring us together as adults. Words cannot describe how rewarding and satisfying and fun it has been to watch my kids excel in their work, to hear them give presentations at meetings and conferences, to have one-on-one dinners with them to discuss business strategy, and to be impressed by their accomplishments. I am especially proud that they have a passion for the food business, a passion that shines through even when they occasionally disagree with one of my suggestions. Like all families, we do have our disagreements, as well as our times of tension and tears. But, as a family, we have persevered through the tough times, and there is every indication that Reser's will remain a family business for many generations to come.

Giving Back

The promise Pat and I made to each other before our wedding that for better, for worse, for richer, for poorer, we would always give back to our community is one that has provided us with a lifetime of enjoyment. In the early years, we focused on our kids' activities. We would buy t-shirts and pay a hundred dollars for fees and sponsor eight or ten little-league baseball teams around the region. As the company grew, so too did our interest in a variety of non-profits. Given Pat's training as a teacher, we have been especially supportive of organizations that support our public schools. One of those organizations is Junior Achievement, which sends volunteers into the classroom to teach our kids about the importance of the private-enterprise system. Reser's support of JA earned me the honor of carrying the 1996 Olympic torch for a mile through the streets of Portland. When I was told I would be a torch bearer, I immediately went into training, as I was having severe knee difficulties at the time. For six weeks, I practiced walking the mile distance while holding a bar that was similar in weight to the torch. When the torch was finally handed to me in the middle of the night, I was so excited that I almost broke into a run. My kids yelled at me to slow down because they didn't think I could make the whole mile at that pace. I took their advice and successfully handed the torch to another runner after completing my mile. Eight back surgeries and knee-replacement surgeries mean that I probably won't be making any more mile-long walks, but it hasn't slowed down Pat's and my commitment to giving back.

We have also taken great satisfaction and pride in the fact that giving back appears to be hereditary. Our five children have all experienced the joy of philanthropy, and one of the best Christmas gifts Pat and I ever received was when our grandchildren informed us that they had made a donation in our name to Heifer International, an organization with a goal of ending world hunger and poverty through self-reliance and sustainability.

The one and only "Mac" McAllister. His wisdom and advice were priceless in helping me during my first years at the helm of Reser's.

Reser's Fine Foods goes public in 1960.

Mom, Dad, Lois, and I inspect some sales figures in the late 1950s.

Lois and family friend and employee Joan Pore toast the conclusion of another successful day.

Caramel apples helped Reser's expand our sales beyond the summer months, but they sure were a sticky mess to make!

The ever-increasing popularity of Mexican food has been instrumental in Reser's growth and success. Today, we produce over five million tortillas each day.

Mark and Al looking over a property in Topeka, Kansas, now home to the Topeka Salad Facility.

Pat and I host a Fourth of July Celebration each year with family and friends. Here we are with the "star of the show" (see page 73) after a long day of creative cooking.

Carrying the 1996 Olympic torch through the streets of Portland was a thrill I will always remember.

Pat and I love to travel. Here we are in Mexico.

Pat is due the lion's share of credit for successfully raising five children who make us proud every day.

Enjoying a quiet moment at a Reser's holiday party. Photo by *Images by Floom*.

My motorized scooter race with fellow food executive Vinny Gruppuso was the talk of an industry convention.

I love parades and was very proud when this Reser's float won the Sweepstakes Award in the 1995 Portland Rose Festival and also won the Sweepstakes Award at the Pasadena Tournament of Roses, 1998.

One title better than Chief Executive Officer is the title of "Grandpa." Here I am with Pat and the grandkids in Mexico in 2010.

SEVEN

O n December 3, 2009, Pat and I traveled to Autzen Stadium in Eugene to watch our Beavers battle the University of Oregon Ducks. All football games are important events for the legion of fans known as "Beaver Nation," but this one was especially crucial. Not only was it the annual "Civil War" game against our arch-rivals, but for the first time in the long history of the rivalry, the game was for all the marbles—or all the roses. Whichever team was victorious would win the Pacific-10 Conference championship and travel to play in the Rose Bowl in Pasadena, California on New Year's Day 2010.

The importance of the game made a Civil War ticket the "must-have" item of the year, and everybody who was anybody in Oregon wanted to be there. How valuable were the tickets? Well, Pat and I donated two seats in the Reser's box along with a limousine ride to the game to Special Olympics of Oregon for their annual fundraising dinner. The tickets were auctioned off for a grand total of ten thousand dollars!

Pat and I traditionally host a tailgate party before most Beaver home games, and even though we were traveling to enemy territory, we did so again. Our tent was overflowing with hundreds and hundreds of our guests—family, friends, Reser's employees, business associates, even Ted

Kulongoski, the Governor of Oregon. The Beavers and the Ducks thrilled the packed stadium and a national television audience with an incredibly exciting and well-played game. As all football fans will know, the Beavers came up on the short end of a 37-33 final score. I remain confident, however, that it won't be long before the Beavers play in Pasadena on New Year's Day. One thing for certain is that Pat and I will be there when it happens.

Just as I am optimistic about the future of the Beavers, I am also optimistic about the future of Reser's Fine Foods. Although it is hard for me to believe, 2010 marks sixty years since my parents began the business in our farmhouse kitchen, and fifty years since I became CEO. While the process of writing this book has allowed me to reflect on the past, I remain much more focused on the future.

The past few years have been tremendously challenging ones for large and small businesses across America, as well as for countless families. I am very proud that we at Reser's have not only kept our heads above water during these times, we have also continued to grow and expand. Americans are always looking for value, and never more so than in times of economic uncertainty, so perhaps it is no surprise that we achieved seven percent sales growth in 2009.

While many businesses would be overjoyed with seven percent sales growth, I expect us to do better. There's an old saying that "the surest way to crush your laurels is to sit on them," and I have made it very clear that Reser's will never be satisfied with sitting still.

For instance, I have set a goal of ten percent annual revenue growth for the foreseeable future. To help achieve this goal, in January of 2010 we announced our plans for expansion of our plant in Halifax, North Carolina. This expansion will increase our presence and our sales in the eastern United States.

No matter how big Reser's gets, we will always remain true to the values, the culture, and the corporate philosophy that I brought with me on my first day as CEO in 1960. It's a philosophy that was first formed during my time playing high-school football, and it has been strengthened by decades of cheering for the Beavers. That philosophy is a belief that every employee of Reser's is a valuable member of a team. And all team members share a great deal in common. We all want a job that is rewarding, challenging, and fun. We all want a job that offers a fair salary and benefits. We all want to build on Reser's reputation for innovation, for state-of-the-art facilities, for developing people, and for caring about our communities.

Just as back in 1960, I could never have imagined what Reser's would look like in 2010, I can't be certain what the company will look like in 2060. But based on our history and our standards and where we are headed in the next several years, I have a pretty good idea of our future. I see new generations of Resers learning and loving the family business. I see a continued commitment to innovation, to quality, and to meeting the needs of our customers. I see that next breakthrough product that will carry us well past the $1 billion annual sales mark. I see employees who enjoy coming to work and who are empowered to do their absolute best. I see countless organizations that are better off because of Reser's commitment to giving back to our community. In short, I see a future where small potatoes and big dreams are still a recipe for success.

EIGHT

I have not yet mentioned one particular characteristic that is helpful to anyone wanting to make a mark in the food business: good taste buds. I'm certainly not a gourmet, but I do know what tastes great and, more importantly, I know what tastes great to America's families. This book wouldn't be complete if I didn't share with you some of my favorite recipes.

"Yellow Paint Sauce" Recipe

In the 1970s, we sold grilled steak sandwiches—a two-ounce beefsteak between two pieces of bread—in the parking lot of many grocery stores. Kids loved it when we would spread our yellow sauce on the sandwiches with a paint brush. We sold thousands of these little sandwiches at the bargain price of ten cents each.

The "yellow paint sauce" is a very secret recipe and extremely difficult to reproduce. It might take a food technologist or a chemist to mix it successfully. If you want to make enough for a whole family or for a picnic barbecue, follow these instructions exactly:

☞ Mix one cup yellow mustard with one cup mayonnaise

Stir vigorously until you achieve a beautiful yellow paint color

Spread generously on sandwich and enjoy!

Dad's Secret Sauce/Dressing

This recipe was developed in the mid-1950s by a company in Los Angeles. I thought it was delicious when I first tasted it, and over the years I was able to duplicate it. It is great as a dressing for salads, on baked potatoes, on steamed vegetables, or as a sandwich spread.

- 1/2 cup sour cream
- 1/4 cup mayonnaise
- 2 tbsp. Worcestershire sauce
- 1 tsp. black pepper
- 1 tsp. chopped garlic (not garlic salt)
- 1 tsp. lemon juice

Mix all ingredients together until well blended. Cover and refrigerate for at least thirty minutes before serving. Enjoy!

Al's Secret Caesar Salad Dressing

Caesar Salad is a mainstay at Reser family gatherings, and my special dressing has been perfected over the years. Our family rule: If one person eats garlic, everyone has to have garlic!

- 2 egg yolks
- 1 cup good olive oil
- 4 cloves of peeled garlic, finely chopped
- Juice of 1 lemon (½ for salad dressing, ½ for lettuce)
- 4 anchovy filets
- 1 tsp. mustard powder
- 1 tbsp. Worcestershire sauce
- 1 tsp. vinegar
- ¼ cup parmesan cheese
- Black pepper to taste

Start by putting yolks in blender. Turn blender on high speed and add olive oil in a slow, steady stream. Turn blender to low speed and add half of the lemon juice and the other remaining ingredients.

Rub a garlic clove on the inside of a wooden bowl. Put Romaine lettuce in the bowl. Pour half of the lemon juice over the lettuce. Add croutons. Pour freshly made dressing on top of the salad. Sprinkle a bit more parmesan cheese on top. What a beautiful salad!

Al's Infamous Chili Hot-Dog Sauce

I thought I had a winner with this sauce, but it never caught on. I still think I was right, and recommend you make some for your next Beaver tailgate party!

2 lbs. cooked ground beef

1/2 cup minced onion

1 tsp. garlic powder

1/2 cup ketchup

1 cup tomato sauce

I tbsp. cider vinegar

1 tbsp. chili powder

Put all ingredients in a bowl and stir to combine.

Line hot dog buns with a steamed or grilled hot dog and top with sauce. Sprinkle with chopped onions and shredded cheese.

The AL-phabet

At our annual sales meetings, I have long tried to motivate our team with inspiring quotations and words of advice. I recently put some of those words together in what I call the "Al-phabet."

A is for attitude. A positive one is a powerful force that can't be stopped.

B is for the Beavers. Pat and I take great pride in the academic and athletic success of Oregon State University.

C is for the customer. If you don't take care of them, somebody else will.

D is for determination. Set a goal and don't stop until you achieve it.

E is for excellence. Strive for it every day.

F is for family. Nothing is more important.

G is for giving back. Find a worthy cause in your community and donate your time, talent, or treasure.

H is for horizon. A good leader keeps an eye on the horizon, not just on the bottom line.

I is for innovation. Innovations have made Reser's an industry leader, and the next innovation will make us a billion dollar business.

J is for job. Find a job that fills you with a sense of passion and you will have found your career.

K is for kitchen. Every kitchen needs a supply of Reser's products!

L is for laughter. It's a necessary ingredient in the recipe for a happy and healthy workplace.

M is for mealtime. Bringing families and friends together for great meals is what Reser's is all about.

N is for nice. Always remember that it's nice to be important, but it's more important to be nice.

O is for optimism. Approach every new situation with it.

P is for potato salad. Were you expecting anything else?

Q is for quality. You can find it in every product we make.

R is for risk. There is risk you cannot afford to take, and there is risk you cannot afford not to take.

S is for success. Some people dream of it, while others wake up and work for it.

T is for teamwork. It's the key to success in sports and in business.

U is for united. Managers and employees must be united behind a common goal.

V is for value. Families need it. Reser's provides it.

W is for wave. If you are not riding the wave of change, you'll find yourself left beneath it.

X is for Xmas. Reser's products have become a tradition at holiday meals.

Y is for yes. It's what you say to your customers.

Z is for zest. Live life with enthusiasm!

Potato Salads

When she was making potato salad in her farmhouse kitchen, my mother could never have dreamed that one day the business she co-founded would make over ninety different potato salads. Here they all are in alphabetical order, and I suppose that some time or other, I've taste-tested them all!

American Harvest Creamy Salad

American Harvest Potato Salad

American Potato Salad

Baked Potato Salad

Baked Potato Salad with Bacon

Caesar Potato Salad
(My newest one, added in 2010)

Canada Red Potato

Cheddar Potato Salad

Chunky Potato Salad

Classic Mustard Potato Salad

Classic Potato Salad

Classic Sliced Potato Salad

Country Potato Salad

Country Style Potato Salad

Country Style Red Potato Salad

Creamy Mustard Potato

Creamy Potato Salad

Creole Potato Salad

Deli Potato Salad

Deluxe Picnic Potato Salad

Deluxe Potato and Egg Salad

Deluxe Potato Salad

Deluxe Red Skin Potato Salad

Deluxe Three Potato Salad

Deviled Egg Potato Salad

Diced American Potato Salad

Diced Potato Salad With Egg

Dill and Caper Salad

Dixie Potato Salad

Farm Style Potato Salad

Fat-Free Red Sliced Potato Salad

German Potato Salad

Golden Gate Potato Salad

Gourmet Mustard Potato Salad

Gourmet Potato Salad

Grandma's Homestyle Potato and Egg Salad

Hawaiian Potato Salad

Hawaiian Potato Mac Salad

Homestyle Potato Salad

Loaded Potato Salad

Mardi Gras Potato Salad

Mustard Potato Salad

Mustard Potato and Egg Salad

New Potato Salad

New Red Bliss Potato Salad

New England Potato Salad

New York Deli Potato Salad

Northwest Potato Salad

Northwest Homestyle Potato Salad

Old Fashioned Potato Salad

Original Potato Salad

Picnic Potato Salad

Potato and Egg Salad

Potato Salad

Potato Salad with Celery Seed

Potato Salad with Egg

Potato Salad with Mayo

Potato Salad with Vegetables

Premium Potato and Egg Salad

Premium Potato Salad

Real Red Potato Salad

Red Bliss Potato Salad

Red Blush Potato Salad

Red Potato Salad with Champagne Vinaigrette

Red Potato Salad with Dill

Red Potato Salad

Red Potato Salad with Sour Cream and Dill

Red Skin Potato Salad

Red Wedge Potato Salad

Red, White, and Blue Potato Salad

Redskin Potato Salad

Regular Mustard Potato Salad

Regular Potato Salad

Royal Blush Potato Salad

Russian Potato Salad

Sliced Potato Salad

Slice Potato Salad with Egg

Southern Mustard Potato Salad

CHAPTER EIGHT

Southern Deluxe Potato Salad with Egg

Southern Potato Salad

Southern Style Potato Salad

Southwest Potato Salad

Texas Potato Salad

Texas Redskin Potato Salad

Three Potato Salad

Trio Potato Salad

Two Mustard Potato Salad

Yellow Mustard Potato Salad

The Oregonian paid tribute to Al in this editorial, which was published on April 16, 2010. (© 2010 The Oregonian. All rights reserved. Used with permission.)

Al Reser's fine life

One of Oregon's most successful businessmen leaves behind a remarkable legacy of generosity.

It's said that no one on a football team is irreplaceable. But Oregon State University—actually, all of Oregon—has lost a man on its team, a guy with two bad knees and a back that hurt all the time, who came as close as one can get.

The man was, of course, Al Reser, the businessman, philanthropist and Beaver Believer who died in his sleep Tuesday at his vacation home in Sarasota, Fla. Reser was 74.

His loss is such a painful blow because Reser was both uncommonly successful in business and uncommonly generous with the money he made. He was the CEO and chairman of Reser's Fine Foods, which he grew from a small family business selling potato salad door to door into an international brand with 2,000 workers and $800 million in annual sales.

Reser shared his financial success with his alma mater (class of 1960) that he loved so much. It was Reser who quarterbacked the funding of new facilities that helped spur the resurgence of the OSU football team, which went from 28 straight losing years to competing for the Rose Bowl, one of the most unlikely turnarounds in college sports. He gave more than $14 million to support the expansion of what is now deservedly known as Reser Stadium.

It wasn't just the football team that benefited from Reser's low-key, humble and generous support. Reser and his wife, Pat, who remains an active OSU fundraiser, gave $10.6 million to the school for the Linus Pauling Science Center and also have donated to a new School of Business building. Outside of OSU, Reser was a major supporter of the Rose Festival Foundation and Special Olympics Oregon.

Interviewed after Reser's death was announced Tuesday, OSU football coach Mike Riley said, "We all knew the impact he's made on our lives. Really, he changed our lives here, totally."

For an OSU man like Al Reser, it's hard to imagine a better legacy.

NO SMALL POTATOES

Allen Avenue Facility; Beaverton, Oregon: One of my first big decisions when I became president of Reser's was to build this 33,000-square-foot facility. Some wondered if we were dreaming too big when we moved there in 1961, but it didn't take long before we needed much more room.

Jenkins Avenue Headquarters and Distribution Center; Beaverton, Oregon: We built our 185,000-square-foot corporate headquarters and production facility in 1971, and added a 40,000-square-foot distribution center in 1985. We have already produced over 1.6 billion pounds of Reser's products at this facility, and look forward to producing many billions more.

Topeka Mexican Food Facility, Topeka, Kansas: I could never have dreamed when I became president of Reser's that one day we would be big enough to build a facility in my home state. Originally built in 1986, the success of our Mexican food line and our refrigerated salad and potato line led to expansions in 1991, 1994, 2003, and 2005. The entire operation is now over 400,000 square feet, produces over 300 million pounds of products and distributes over 24 million cases of products annually.

Topeka Salad Facility, Topeka, Kansas: In 1991, the Topeka Salad Facility was built to help us meet the needs of our customers in the mid-West. The plant was initially 56,000 square feet of production and distribution space. Over the past 19 years, and through multiple expansions, it has grown to just over 200,000 square feet and produces over 125,000,000 pounds of salad, salsa, desserts, and side dishes annually.

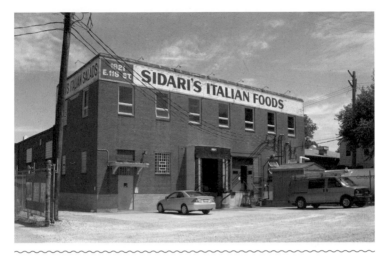

Cleveland Facility, Cleveland, Ohio: When we purchased Sidari's Italian Foods in 1992, we purchased a company that makes some of the nation's best pasta, salads, and other Italian food products.

Hawaii Facility, Kaneohe, Hawaii: We acquired our Aloha State facility when we purchased Hawaiian Eateries Salads in 1993. Come winter, everyone in our Oregon headquarters wants to find an excuse to pay a visit here!

Pasco Facility; Pasco, Washington: This 110,000-square-foot facility, built in 1999, is located right in the heart of potato country, ensuring our potato products are the freshest in the market.

Halifax Facility, Halifax, North Carolina: The purchase of a number of companies in the eastern United States led to us building this facility in North Carolina in 2001.

Salt Lake City Facility, Salt Lake, Utah: With the purchase of Lynn Wilson Foods in 2002, we acquired this 70,000-square-foot facility, which produces excellent Mexican foods.

Don Pancho Facility, Salem, Oregon: This facility in Oregon's capital city was acquired in 2003, and annually produces 70 million pounds of Mexican food products.

Deer Creek Facility, Topeka, Kansas: The Deer Creek Facility, at 193,000 square feet, is our largest volume production plant and will produce upwards of 170,000,000 pounds of side dishes and fresh potatoes this year, servicing markets from Denver to the East Coast.

Don Pancho Mexican Foods Plant, Halifax, North Carolina: In 2010, we will begin operation of our newest plant—shown here in an artist's rendering. The state-of-the-art facility will produce multiple varieties of corn and flour tortillas for the East Coast. This plant will have more than 81,000 square feet, with room for expansion.

Aerial view of Reser Stadium, 2008. Photo by University Marketing, Oregon State University

Reser Stadium's field of play, with crowds of enthusiastic fans packing the stands.

ACKNOWLEDGEMENTS

I have learned that writing a book is like running a business—you can't do it without a great team. This book would not have been possible without the assistance and advice of many individuals.

I begin by thanking Margie Hunt. Margie is the CEO of Oregon Special Olympics, which is a truly inspiring organization and one of my favorite charitable causes. It was Margie who told me on numerous occasions that I should share the story of Reser's and that Kerry Tymchuk was just the person to help me do that. She was right about Kerry, and I have enjoyed our many sessions together and thank him for his help in making this book a reality.

This book would not have become a reality without the assistance of the most valued and trusted Mari Jo Prlain. Keeping me on schedule is just one of the countless jobs performed to perfection for many years by Mari Jo. She was involved in this process at every step of the way, and her unbelievable memory and wise suggestions were invaluable throughout the writing process.

Finally, I wish that in this book I could have told stories about every individual who played a role in Reser's success. Had I done so, however, the book would have been heavier than a sack of potatoes. Here are the names of a number of current and former managers and employees who were not mentioned in the book, but to whom I am indebted for sharing their talents with Reser's.

Norm Price, John Sinner, Gary Wills, Paul Leavy, and Diana Robertson have been the "number crunchers"— the controllers and chief financial officers who made sure the books balanced.

Ollie Jacques, Harvey Reser, Jerry Reser, Steve Parmelee, Stan Rowland, Glen Knippenberg, Jack Durett, Terry Stewart, Ron Leeper, Peter Sirgy, Ralph Thackery, Jack Bean, Jack Romaine, Jim Denton, Don Krahmer, Bud Lents, George Hankin, Dave Hume, Darren Jones, and Ricardo Baez are representative of the talented and hardworking individuals who have served as salesmen and sales managers.

Tony Kunis, Jana Taylor, Sue Deeming, Barbara Jordan, Randy Earle, Michael Harding, Jeff Adair, Rob Wiskerchen, Jeff Russell, Karen Schenk, Ralph and Carol Riggs, Steve Loehndorf, Tammie DeBardardin, Jerry Coates, Mike Conners, Ronda Farber, Thor Wentzek, Chet Smith, Bruce Jensen, Adam Babcock, Brad Pacey, Bennie Aleshire, Jake Ragland, Steve Snyder, George Puentes, Lynn Stevens: Whether it's plant operations, research and development, office management, purchasing, human resources, or quality control, all of these individuals helped to write many chapters in the history of Reser's.

ACKNOWLEDGEMENTS

To all Reser's employees—past, present, and future—I say: from the time our company was founded we have been committed to creating and fostering an environment where outstanding people like you can accomplish extraordinary results. We are in a business where people make the difference, and where initiative, teamwork, and talent open doors to success. Thank you for making that difference for Reser's. I look forward to working with you and to many more years of success.

The best part of running a family business is family. Pat and I are joined here by our five children (left to right, Mike, Marty, Mindy, Michelle, Mark) at the Jenkins Headquarters in 1997. Photo by *Images by Floom.*